BRAIN GAMES

Crosswords

pil

Publications International, Ltd.

Puzzle Consultants: Adam Cohen, Julie K. Cohen, Shawn Kennedy, Amy Reynaldo

Puzzle Constructors: Deb Amlen, Patrick Blindauer, Kelly Clark, Mark Danna, Gayle Dean, Harvey Estes, Ray Hamel, Tyler Hinman, Matt Jones, Roy Leban, John McCarthy, Fred Piscop, Brendan Quigly, Wayne Robert Williams

Illustrators: Helem An, Chris Gattorna, Elizabeth Gerber, Robin Humer, Shavan Spears, Jen Torche

Cover Puzzles: Mark Danna, Ray Hamel

Cover Image: Shutterstock.com

Follow the Clues!

The fountain of youth may only exist in fairy tales, but that has done nothing to stop the search for secrets to health and longevity. Of course, it's hardly a secret that one way to stay young and live a fulfilling life is to keep our bodies and minds in shape. Eating right and working out takes care of the body, but how can we stay cognitively fit?

The answer to that question can be easy and fun. Many gerontologists and physicians recommend working puzzles as a way of retaining mental fitness. Puzzles increase mental flexibility, demand focused attention, and require the use of problem-solving skills, all of which are important cognitive functions. We might think of puzzles as mini brain workouts.

Brain Games®: Crosswords is full of such mini brain workouts—more than 80 of them—for people who love to play with words. The puzzles have varying levels of difficulty—from Very Easy to Difficult to Expert—to keep you on your toes. So use your mental muscle and add to your vocabulary as you figure out these clues and solutions. If any of the puzzles stump you completely, the answers are conveniently located in the back of the book.

Flip to the next page and get started! Working out your brain has never been so intriguing—and fun!

1 | Which Way Is Which?

ACROSS

1. "Clash of the Titans" goddess
5. Cobbler's hole maker
8. You don't want to hear this from your barber
12. "Mr. Holland's _____"
13. _____ polloi
14. Ancient alphabetical character
15. Progressive faction
17. Home of the Jazz
18. Put off
19. Put your arms around and squeeze
21. Deodorant brand
27. Bruin Hall of Famer Bobby
30. "_____ Te Ching"
31. Capital of French Indochina
32. Piglet's friend
34. Drive bananas
36. Majesty preceder
37. Standoffish
39. Quick drink
41. Snood
42. Kept secret
45. To and _____
46. Puccini opera set in Rome
50. Brazos River city
53. "Stat!"
56. Fair word?
57. Make an attempt
58. Gutter spot
59. "Sesame Street" character
60. Dress bottom
61. Traveled quickly

DOWN

1. "_____ on Tight" (ELO hit)
2. Sporting blade
3. Dennis the Menace's dog
4. Sunflower relative
5. Sushi bar tuna
6. Was crowned champion
7. Not weighing much
8. Montevideo's country
9. Word after Pizza and Sunglass in company names
10. "I met him _____ Monday..." (song lyric)
11. Laugh sound
16. Order
20. Kin of "yuck"
22. "_____-Jin" (James Clavell bestseller)

23. They may beep
24. Directly
25. Immoralist
26. Surface of some tracks or roads
27. Birthstone after sapphire
28. Hamlet or Ophelia
29. "Up on the ____" (1962 Drifters hit)
33. Fiery practical joke
35. Spectra maker
38. Sable or mink
40. Sun-hat material
43. Where snowbirds head in spring
44. Lavishes affection (on)
47. Pass to the quarterback
48. Shoreline recess
49. Amazed
50. Fly catcher
51. Lumberjack's tool
52. Lesson for an EMT
54. More than vexation
55. School assembly locale, perhaps

2 | Ma Chérie

ACROSS

1. Paint-can instruction
5. Massage facility
8. Architect's diagram
12. Simple road
13. Candy in a collectible dispenser
14. Insubstantial
15. _____-deucey (game)
16. Price to participate
18. Tell-all about Joan Crawford
20. Cut out
21. Dance bit?
22. Marshy area
25. Answering machine button
27. Pre-weekend letters
31. Inlay material
35. Stop order?
36. Baby's syllable
37. It's up there
38. Army cops: abbr.
41. Associate of Larry and Curly
43. 1948 film starring Irene Dunne
50. Salad bar item
51. High point
52. Crude cartel
53. Counterpart of long.
54. Tea leaf reader's opening
55. Die, with "out"
56. Med. drama sets
57. Land parcels

DOWN

1. E-promotions, e.g.
2. Folded lunch
3. Gossip column offering
4. Sample for example?
5. Road menace
6. Be in limbo
7. Tlaloc worshipper
8. It rises when you get a raise
9. Magazine founded in 1936
10. Belligerent Olympian
11. Duma dissent
17. Sidelines shout
19. About, in legalese
22. Z3 automaker
23. Surprised cry
24. Certain Pontiac

26. Gear part
28. Nitrous oxide, e.g.
29. Bother
30. Tsetse, for one
32. Swinging bed
33. Works up
34. Inferior
39. Writing instrument
40. Winner's look
42. Modern missive

43. High-performance Camaro model
44. Nonpayment consequence
45. Place of bliss
46. Wild pig
47. Lhasa _____ (dog breed)
48. Comply with
49. Forest hackers

3 | Not True!

ACROSS
1. Lassie, e.g.
4. Worker's pay
8. Civil insurrection
12. Praise-filled poem
13. "Zounds!"
14. Mountain reverberation
15. "Not true!"
18. Nabisco cookies
19. Pig's place
20. Female deer
21. Mel of baseball
23. Large body of water
25. Male adults
28. "Dig in!"
30. Epistle writer
34. "Not true!"
38. 1950s actress Arlene
39. Skillet, e.g.
40. Mom's mate
41. Central
44. Traditional dessert
46. Unruly hair
49. Restaurant bill
51. Physicist Enrico
55. "Not true!"
58. Poison ivy symptom
59. False god
60. "Silent _____"
    (Coolidge's nickname)
61. Jot down
62. Certain
63. "Grand _____ Opry"

DOWN
1. Numbskull
2. Dumpster emanation
3. Dancer/actor/singer Kelly
4. Noah of dictionary fame
5. Grow older
6. Dates for guys
7. Cuts text, maybe
8. Christian clerical title: abbr.
9. Chilled
10. Columbus is its capital
11. Carry
16. Also
17. Needle hole
22. Beige-colored
24. Big galoot
25. Wet dirt
26. Airport letters
27. To the _____ degree
29. T-shirt, e.g.

31. Common conjunction
32. Red, white, and blue letters
33. Directed
35. Common street name
36. 40 winks
37. Cold symptom
42. "_____ a boy!" (delivery room cry)
43. Smears paint
45. Moray or conger

46. Primary
47. Herr Bismarck
48. Ancient Scot
50. Boyfriend
52. Puerto _____
53. Lunch, e.g.
54. Small land in the water
56. "_____ Loves You" (early Beatles hit)
57. Rowboat need

4 | Celebrity Crossword

ACROSS

1. Odds and ends: abbr.
5. "Fear and Loathing in _____ Vegas" (1998)
8. Cherrystone, e.g.
12. Limburger quality
13. Manning of the Giants
14. Longest Swiss river
15. "_____ Want to Do" (Sugarland song)
16. "Delta of Venus" author Anaïs
17. Small mattress size
18. Liam in "Taken"
20. Jackson in "Nasty Habits"
22. Player under contract
23. High tennis shot
24. Robin Hood's maid
27. Queen of mysteries
31. Lena in "Chocolat"
32. "Video" singer India._____
33. Steven in "Under Siege"
36. Costa Rica neighbor
38. Untruth
39. Tolkien monster
40. Playwright Pinter
43. Ernest Borgnine TV role

47. Tel _____
48. Generation _____
50. "East of Eden" director Kazan
51. Courtney of Hole
52. "Able was I _____ . . ."
53. Hit the horn
54. Lollapalooza
55. 2016 Olympics city
56. Perfect scores

DOWN

1. Banshee wail
2. "Monty Python" regular Eric
3. Dover fish
4. "Hot Tub Time Machine" costar
5. Fab Four member
6. Muhammad or Laila
7. Marital status
8. "Robin Hood" actress
9. Something to mow
10. Like Death Valley
11. Suvari in "American Beauty"
19. "Are you a man _____ mouse?"
21. Online "ha-ha": abbr.

	1	2	3	4		5	6	7		8	9	10	11
	12					13				14			
	15					16				17			
	18				19			20	21				
				22				23					
	24	25	26					27			28	29	30
	31									32			
	33				34	35		36	37				
				38				39					
	40	41	42					43			44	45	46
	47					48	49			50			
	51					52				53			
	54					55				56			

24. _____ Def in "The Italian Job"
25. Pub pint
26. River inlet
28. CC Sabathia stat
29. Outer edge
30. A vote "for"
34. Feel crummy
35. Heath in "The Dark Knight"
36. Ellen of "Grey's Anatomy"
37. Smiley mouth
40. 2009 Beyoncé hit
41. Stratford river
42. Tear apart
44. Spiny African plant
45. Aslan, for one
46. Chows down
49. Gold of "Entourage"

5 | Book 'Em!

ACROSS

1. Atomizer output
5. Member of Jason's crew
13. Chip in
14. Legible, as in handwriting
15. Glance over
16. Set off
17. First printing, often
19. Side squared, for a square
20. Hang over one's head
24. Specialists in storytelling?
28. Island near Singapore
30. Stir up
32. Bandleader Cugat
33. Event where a mosh pit may form
35. Smart-mouthed
36. Deep _____ bend
37. Alleviate
39. Printing after 17-Across
44. Logged on, in a way
48. Crazy as a _____
49. Gun manufacturers
50. Chinese leader?
51. She might feed your baby for you
52. _____ moss

DOWN

1. Radar unit?
2. Machu Picchu builder
3. Hollywood's "Walk of Fame" feature
4. Care for
5. Hot blood
6. Keanu of "The Matrix"
7. Cakes in Cannes
8. Carbon monoxide's lack
9. Bread served with korma
10. Attorneys' grp.
11. Final: abbr.
12. Course requirement?
18. Hindu social division
20. _____ lamp
21. Elevator inventor
22. Loads from lodes
23. "Pietà" figure
24. Canine kiss
25. _____ a secret

26. Bad spots?
27. Wild _____
29. Electromagnetic wave enhancer
31. Nook or Kindle
34. Long-snouted, piglike critters
38. It may be common
39. Lima's locale

40. Radar screen image
41. Blue-ribbon
42. End piece
43. Gut feeling?
44. Tool with teeth
45. Boiling blood
46. Clock standard: abbr.
47. _____ compos mentis

6 | Greek to Me

ACROSS

1. "_____ Maria"
4. Cry like a baby
8. Affirm
12. Flipper
13. Waikiki wingding
14. In the buff
15. TV monitor?
16. Barbershop request
17. Novelist Bagnold
18. Flight data: abbr.
20. Leader of the pack
22. Receipt listings
24. Mogadishu resident
25. Halloween handout
26. Scoundrel
27. Filmmaker Spike
28. VHS alternative, once
31. Ghost's cry
34. Allow
35. Doctrine
39. "The Little Mermaid" villainess
41. Gung-ho
42. Atomic nucleus emission
45. Jellystone Park denizen
46. Squishy lump
47. Seize suddenly
49. Pique
50. "If all _____ fails..."
51. Ethereal
52. Capitol Hill VIP
53. Textile worker
54. Fit to be tried
55. Big Apple attraction, with "the"

DOWN

1. Change
2. Spoils recipient
3. Package
4. Counter offer?
5. Ambience
6. Sing the blues
7. The whole shebang, money-wise
8. Perpendicular to the keel
9. Home wrecker
10. Baltimore ballplayer
11. Uncomfortable underclothing condition
19. Try
21. "Satires" author

23. Stanley's wife in "A Streetcar Named Desire"
26. Jazz man, slangily
29. One way to quell a riot
30. Look into?: hyph.
31. Annoyed
32. How most medications are taken
33. Diffuse slowly

36. Self-absorption
37. One of 90 in a right angle
38. Set straight
40. Brownish
43. "O mio babbino caro," e.g.
44. Kitten's plaything
48. "See ya!"

7 | In Touch with the Feminine Side

ACROSS

1. Alternatives to Macs
4. Treasure holder
9. Poke fun at
12. Former coach Parseghian
13. Golfer's dream
15. "In Touch" "Sideways" actor?
17. Naysayer
18. King of the macabre
19. Think advisable
22. Spill the beans
23. Pencil topper
27. ACLU concern
28. "In Touch" "Munich" actor?
30. Partner of games
32. Many a church is named for her
33. _____ Domini
35. Expressed pain
39. Some piano keys
43. Two-tone cookie
44. "In Touch" "Taxi Driver" actor?
47. Dishonestly obtained
48. Berliner's article
49. Summer in Québec
50. Cozy places
51. Rudy or Sandra

DOWN

1. Mama's mates
2. Construction site hoist
3. Cook in butter
4. Chinese tea
5. Take more than your share of
6. New Haven collegians
7. Senate position
8. "Stop the clock!"
9. Type of nest egg
10. Purpose
11. Earthlings and ETs
14. Kindergarten breaks
16. Career soldier
20. Eye part

	1	2	3		4	5	6	7	8		9	10	11
12					13					14			
15			16										
17						18							
19				20	21				22				
		23			24	25	26		27			
	28							29				
30	31			32								
33			34			35		36	37	38
39				40	41	42		43			
44						45	46				
47								48			
49				50					51			

21. White lie, sometimes
24. Fictional detective Spade
25. Online auction site
26. Highly unusual
28. Lend dignity to
29. Hose material
30. Spencer's "The _____ Queene"
31. Open, as a deadlock

34. Blood type, briefly
36. Meddled
37. Frightfully strange
38. Cookie package word
40. It's pumped at a gym
41. Ending for Jean or Ann
42. College entrance exams: abbr.
45. NYPD rank
46. Halves of ems

8 | But First, an Aperitif!

ACROSS

1. Liqueur sometimes served with three coffee beans as garnish
8. Filch
13. Delighted
14. Not plus
15. Veteran
16. Montezuma, e.g.
17. Little piggy
18. Affix a brand to
20. Victorian, for one
21. Candy best known for its square fruit chews
24. Puppy's bite
25. Old what's-_____-name
26. Table tennis racket
28. Cream cheese holder
31. Schlemiel
32. Historical records
34. Doctor's charge
35. Class-conscious group?: abbr.
36. Made understandable
41. Anderson's "High _____"
42. Assist, in a way
43. Fraternity letter
44. Coastal feature
46. Harry of "This Is Spinal Tap" fame
49. Prolonged attack
50. Nuttier
51. Foofaraws
52. _____ International (human rights watchdogs)

DOWN

1. Dalmatian marks
2. Apportion
3. Euripides drama
4. "_____, humbug!"
5. It's a free country: abbr.
6. Population count
7. Venomous viper
8. Wise guy
9. "Nobody beats the _____!"
10. Has in mind
11. Childish
12. Slipper?

19. Cleopatra biter
22. Perlman of "Cheers"
23. Microsoft founder
27. Active one
28. John, notably
29. Composer Vivaldi
30. All knotted up
33. Blubber
34. Comprehend

37. Electronics pioneer Nikola
38. Root used in gin-making
39. Quickie ghost costume
40. "My bad!"
45. I problem?
47. Ages and ages
48. King Kong, e.g.

9 | For the Record

ACROSS

1. Con game's victim
5. On the _____ (fleeing)
8. Cy Young has the most in MLB history
12. _____ vera
13. Single
14. Square footage
15. Barry Bonds has the most in MLB history
17. Doe's baby
18. Muscle definition
19. Mimic
21. Cut and paste
24. Coffee allure
28. Undergrad degs.
30. Fly like an eagle
32. _____ capita income
33. Joe DiMaggio has the longest in MLB history
36. Brouhaha
37. Fig. on a baseball card
38. Industrious bug
39. High-strung
41. Put through a sieve
43. Prankster's missile
45. Right-hand person
48. "Ali _____ and the Forty Thieves"

51. Walter Johnson has the most in MLB history
55. Astronaut Shepard
56. "For _____ a jolly..."
57. Granny
58. Pete Rose has the most in MLB history
59. Verily
60. Hit hard

DOWN

1. _____-jongg
2. "Thanks _____!"
3. Cowboys QB Tony
4. Most perceptive
5. Manager Piniella
6. Raggedy doll
7. Flat formation
8. Necco candy piece
9. "Michael Collins" grp.
10. Not old
11. _____ Diego
16. Crimson
20. Go splitsville
22. "Money _____ everything!"
23. Frat party wear
25. Not closed
26. Vegan's no-no

27. Genesis boat
28. _____ one's time (wait)
29. "This must weigh _____!"
31. Italian bubbly
33. Bonnet, for example
34. Words of understanding
35. GI food
40. Stretches across
42. Jack Sprat's taboo
44. Visibly pale

46. Like a Jekyll-Hyde personality
47. Sicilian spewer
48. "Balderdash!"
49. He dethroned Foreman
50. Night flyer
52. Front end of a bray
53. Springsteen's "Born in the _____"
54. "Casablanca" pianist

10 | Romantic Reads

ACROSS

1. Lift a load
5. EMT expertise
8. Improvisational singing style
12. Crunchy ice cream flavor
13. _____ Speedwagon
14. Traveling tramp
15. Snack options
17. Water pitcher
18. Harlequin line of Christian romances
20. Stinging insect
21. Acorn's origin point
22. Singer James
25. "Diamond" lady
26. "To Kill a Mockingbird" state: abbr.
29. Harlequin line of romantic manga
33. Understand
34. _____ Mahal
35. Thumbs-up
36. Prefix with sphere or corn
37. Result of addition
39. Harlequin line of African American romances

44. Attire
45. Reduce
47. At any time
48. Have yet to pay
49. Offering from Pavarotti
50. Astronaut grp.
51. Roll of cash
52. Cracker, of sorts

DOWN

1. Make like a rabbit
2. Makes a mistake
3. Poetic measures
4. Free gift, in some promotions
5. Thin pancake
6. _____ Grant (college financial aid source)
7. Perfume ingredient
8. Arab patriarch
9. Type of sweater neck
10. Ill-fated Biblical brother
11. Craggy mountain peak
16. End of a quiz?
19. Angelic symbol
22. Bird-to-be
23. Allegiance

24. Cable channel that's a blast?
25. JFK's veep
26. Set the price at
27. Mauna _____
28. Poehler of "Parks and Recreation"
30. Lab item
31. Sky colors
32. In the unspecified future
36. Planetary shadow
37. Caught sight of
38. It might be bookmarked
39. Intoxicating Polynesian quaff
40. Gets one's dander up
41. Caucus state
42. Achy
43. Big drink
44. Atty. _____
46. Kvetch

11 | From Stage to Screen

ACROSS

1. "In the Valley of _____"
5. Edge
8. Actress Adams in "The Honey Pot"
12. Tempo
13. _____ Annie, "Oklahoma!" character
14. Shoe bottom
15. Jane Austen novel made into a 1996 movie
16. Matthew's Gospel sung
18. Film critic Roger
20. "Lend me an _____!"
21. 2006 movie musical of 3 ladies with Detroit soul
27. Noticeable opening
30. Molina and Molinaro
31. Bluish-green shade
32. Claire in "Ninotchka"
33. Actress ZaSu in the movie musical "Dames"
36. Ms. Perón in "Evita"
37. Social rebuff
39. Astaire-Rogers musical, "Flying Down to _____"
40. "The Pajama Game" star Doris
41. Babs starred in this 1969 movie songfest

45. Bruins great Bobby
46. Water stop
50. 1936 Hammerstein movie musical
55. _____ of the above
56. Charlie Chaplin prop
57. Moving need
58. Outdoor toy
59. Lab assistant in "Young Frankenstein"
60. Wolf down
61. Food fit for pigs

DOWN

1. Fencer's blade
2. Gyro meat
3. Wile E.'s favorite firm
4. Got the message
5. "Nowadays / Hot Honey _____" number from "Chicago"
6. Wedding vow
7. Online connector
8. _____ de corps
9. Bambi's mate
10. "_____ be back," from "The Terminator"
11. Flotsam or Jetsam in "The Little Mermaid"
17. Professional actors' org.

19. "The Tender _____"
    (with Frank Sinatra)
22. Actor Wallach
23. Houston ballplayer
24. Clarinet insert
25. Flowing rock
26. Dispatch, as in a dragon
27. Lillian of silent pictures
28. "Rachel Getting
    Married" star Hathaway
29. One of the Beatles
34. "Shop _____ you drop"
35. "Star Wars" smuggler
38. Snow remover

42. Spherical form
43. Took the wheel
44. Gives a hard pull
47. Loam or clay
48. "_____ the Night" (1985
    Jeff Goldblum movie)
49. Trickle or drip
50. "Star Trek" genre,
    _____-fi
51. Hardly a beauty
52. Inspiration for Lennon's
    "Woman"
53. One step away from MLB
54. Explosive, briefly

12 | Fit to Be Tied

ACROSS

1. Expression of wonderment
4. Approval of a comic
8. Atty. General's cabinet division
11. "The Jungle Book" snake
12. Combination of protons, neutrons, and electrons
13. Look amazed
14. Play double Dutch
16. John Steinbeck's "East of _____"
17. Raconteur's stock-in-trade
19. Diaper, in Soho
21. Evaluate, as ore
22. End of Jack Horner's boast
23. Two-faced
26. Face impending danger
32. Young dragonfly
33. Tiny drink
34. Up till now
37. Agronomists' study
39. Often on the bench
43. Banjoist Scruggs
44. Basic
47. Antelopes, to lions
48. Deft
49. Stylistically imitative of
50. Long-faced
51. Tournament passes
52. Azure expanse

DOWN

1. Agrees to
2. Sturdy furniture material
3. Kind of sharp turn
4. Flying predator of Greek myth
5. High on
6. Snake dancers
7. Act of Contrition finale
8. Tots' pops
9. "Tosca," e.g.
10. "_____ from the Block," Lopez song
13. Spewing hot spring
15. Chirp
18. Wound deeply
19. "No dice"
20. Org. for doctors

23. Casual memo letters
24. Driver's org.
25. British Inc.
27. Like an old tree trunk
28. Tribal minstrel
29. Inexplicable
    occurrences
30. Feel poorly
31. Infield coups: abbr.
34. Ways up

35. Family name in "Gone
    with the Wind"
36. Put in a kiln
37. Slaw, fries, etc.
38. Single
40. Swedish auto
41. Frozen dessert chain
42. Smoker's sound
45. Similar type
46. Small island

13 | Echoes

ACROSS

1. Banana cover
5. Off-base illegally
9. Pecs' neighbors
12. BBs and bullets, e.g.
13. Skirt length
14. Brazilian vacation destination, for short
15. 1980s detective TV series
18. Copy editor's bane
19. Lord's mate
20. Menacing
23. Cooking amt.
26. Flimflam
29. Biblical woman
30. Hooded winter jacket
31. Repeatedly
34. Flash of light
35. Late columnist Landers
36. Cable channel
37. Hand-in-the-door reaction
38. Tiananmen Square, for one
40. Toothed wheel
42. Scat singer Fitzgerald
45. In circles
50. Solo in "Star Wars"
51. Not natural, for hair
52. "Render therefore _____ Caesar…"
53. Nods, perhaps
54. Former JFK sights
55. Lecturer's platform

DOWN

1. Mas' mates
2. Send out, as energy
3. TV award
4. Belt holders
5. Dr.'s org.
6. Be victorious
7. How eccentrics behave
8. Bart Simpson's sibling
9. Base boy, perhaps
10. Book jacket blurb, often
11. Bart, to Homer
16. Harmful
17. Name holder at a convention
21. An ex of Artie
22. Of the kidneys
24. Scrape, as a knee
25. Show windedness

26. Clever
27. Come-hither look
28. Carpentry tools
30. WWII tank
32. Done permanently, as writing
33. Modern-day evidence
38. Supplicates
39. How storybooks are often read

41. Includes
43. Colorful moth
44. "Nay!" sayer
45. Letter used as a density symbol
46. Sturdy tree
47. Tennis court divider
48. Orthodontist's deg.
49. Shindigs

14 | A Night at the Movies

ACROSS

1. Gang's domain
5. "The Hangover" dentist
8. Streisand, to friends
12. Winglike
13. Drop the ball
14. Bruins of the Pac-12: abbr.
15. Ballet bend
16. "_____ for Silence" (Grafton novel)
17. 1982 Disney sci-fi film
18. "The Blind Side" Oscar winner
21. DeLuise in "Blazing Saddles"
22. Rocker Jerry _____ Lewis
23. Patrick in "Dirty Dancing"
26. Brody in "Splice"
30. "Eureka!"
31. NL or AL award
32. "Leaving _____" (1992)
36. Harvest machine
39. Jack Benny's was "39"
40. Henley rower
41. "Killers" star
48. Start a poker game
49. Neither here _____ there
50. "Guitar _____" (video game)
51. Moore in "The Joneses"
52. Mork's planet
53. "Layla" singer Clapton
54. Stretch across
55. Memphis-Chicago dir.
56. Give off fumes

DOWN

1. Sean Penn's first film
2. "The Producers" secretary
3. "A Day Without _____" (Enya song)
4. "A Nightmare on Elm Street" villain
5. Cookie Monster's street
6. Chicago paper, for short
7. Andress in "Dr. No"
8. Gerard in "The Bounty Hunter"
9. Word form for "high"
10. Political coalition
11. Made a putt
19. Frasier Crane's producer

	1	2	3	4		5	6	7		8	9	10	11
	12					13				14			
	15					16				17			
	18				19				20				
			21					22					
	23	24	25					26			27	28	29
	30										31		
	32			33	34	35		36	37	38			
			39					40					
	41	42	43				44				45	46	47
	48					49				50			
	51					52				53			
	54					55				56			

20. Went first
23. _____ Antonio
24. "_____ Cares?" (Gershwin tune)
25. Berne river
27. Little troublemaker
28. Robot in "WALL-E"
29. "Fresh Air" network: abbr.
33. Marlee of "The West Wing"
34. Back in time
35. "Imagine" singer

36. Mickey in "Iron Man 2"
37. Put away
38. Anne in "Patriot Games"
41. Does the math
42. Leak slowly
43. Mie in "You Only Live Twice"
44. "Freak on a Leash" group
45. Roll-call response
46. One of HOMES
47. Hudson in "Giant"

15 | Crossword for Dummies

ACROSS

1. Prima donna
5. Chemical banned in the U.S. in 1972
8. Male clotheshorses
12. Surpassed
14. Dog in "Garfield"
15. One who works with a dummy
17. Superlative ending
18. Bankbook increase: abbr.
19. Wrist bones
20. Slow run
21. _____ Moines, Iowa
22. Cry from a roller coaster
25. Stage signal
26. Shriner's topper
29. Game played with a dummy
33. Sporty Pontiac model
34. Start for Quentin or Diego
35. Skillet metal
36. Long-jawed fish
37. Mai _____
39. Western African nation
42. Big donating org.
43. Belittle, slangily
46. It involves putting a dummy in a car

49. Not fat
50. Common school fund-raiser, once
51. Be misanthropic
52. Org. with many examiners
53. Kind of school

DOWN

1. White bird
2. Currier's partner
3. Air duct
4. Gallery showing
5. "Nothing _____!" ("No way!")
6. Oaf
7. Potential fight ender
8. Sports no-nos
9. One-eyed Norse god
10. Leaning Tower city
11. Hardens, as concrete
13. Tony Orlando and Dawn, e.g.
16. Unusually different
20. Fighter plane
21. Name
22. Move back and forth, as a finger
23. Simple abode

24. Prefix with system
25. "The Situation Room" network
26. HST's predecessor
27. Self-importance
28. School of Buddhism
30. Bartender on "The Love Boat"
31. Boat mover
32. Number on a grandfather clock
36. Garden statue

37. Pieces of work
38. Stomach trouble
39. Knife cut
40. _____ hoop
41. Fighting
42. Former host of "The Tonight Show"
43. Letter opener?
44. Remote getaway
45. Put one's foot down?
47. Baseball stat
48. One-third of a tbsp.

16 | Say "I Do"

ACROSS

1. British colony until 1970
5. Carrier to Amsterdam: abbr.
8. Momma's boy
12. Sound of an explosion
13. Card game with forfeits
14. Denny's competitor, for short
15. Keen on, slangily
16. Have no accomplices
18. Say "I do"
20. Strengths
23. Schwarz of toys
24. Popeye's greens
26. Broadcast
29. Say "I do"
33. Wood used to make guitars
34. Lifted
35. Tanning lotion abbr.
38. Atlas blowups
39. Say "I do"
43. Trilogy option, maybe
44. Blade with a bell guard
48. Use the pool
49. Big export from Sri Lanka
50. Edibles with shells
51. Squares at diner tables
52. Not unlikely
53. Where to spend kips

DOWN

1. Org. on "The X-Files"
2. Solar wind particle
3. Smidgen
4. Comedienne Coca
5. Gossipy gathering
6. _____ Ness Monster
7. Wallpaper design
8. Word after "roger"
9. "Here comes trouble!"
10. Sound measure
11. Floored it
17. _____ stroke (immediately)
19. Place for a coup
20. Hammett dog
21. Purveyors of pampering
22. Punjab sect member
25. Little chuckle

1	2	3	4		5	6	7		8	9	10	11
12					13				14			
15					16		17					
		18	19									
20	21	22					23					
24					25				26	27	28	
29						30	31	32				
33					34							
		35	36	37		38						
39	40	41			42							
43								44	45	46	47	
48					49				50			
51					52				53			

26. Chips in the pot
27. "And this is the thanks
    _____?"
28. Wine-list choices
30. Indicate
31. Brit's flooring
32. J. P. Morgan co. based
    in Pittsburgh
35. Leaf stalks

36. A degree of success?
37. Italian holiday
39. Recipe shortening?
40. Illinois neighbor
41. Off-ramp
42. Hang on to
45. Tiger's grp.
46. Self-esteem
47. Baron ender

EASY

ACROSS

1. Brewpub lineup
5. Evidence of an eruption
8. Speedy
12. Oratorio number
13. "You don't say!"
14. Like a black olive
15. A comfort food
17. "The doctor _____"
18. One of 2 lines in hangman
19. Fur trader's items
20. Ward off
24. Treats like dirt
26. Oscar winner Sorvino
27. Salon sound
28. With 30-Across, a comfort food
30. See 28-Across
35. Hershey's morsel
37. Subtle glow
38. Cosby's "fat" kid
41. Sneak up slowly
42. Rap sheet name
43. Revlon spokesperson Mendes
45. "The Mod Squad" role
46. A comfort food
51. "Go back," on a PC
52. Pharmaceutical giant _____ Lilly
53. Twiddling one's thumbs
54. Ill-tempered
55. Thieves' retreat
56. Monopoly card

DOWN

1. Mai _____
2. Compass doodle
3. Chart shape
4. Amniotic _____
5. Golden-_____ (senior)
6. One on deck
7. Do some tailoring
8. A comfort food
9. Seating selection
10. Barbecue accessories
11. Perfect scores, at times
16. Mob hit victim, perhaps
19. _____ platter (Chinese appetizer)
20. Part of a rock concert stage
21. Compete
22. "The end of an _____"

23. Turned tail
25. Diners' protectors
27. Recipe step
29. Islands strings
31. Surfacing need
32. When Mardi Gras falls: abbr.
33. Bard's before
34. Grammys category
36. 1980s TV's "Remington _____"

38. Roomy garment: hyph.
39. Blair of "The Exorcist"
40. A comfort food
41. Victim of curiosity
42. Grad
44. Full of oneself
46. RX item, for short
47. Coffee-to-go need
48. "To a . . ." work
49. Ginger _____
50. G-man, e.g.

ACROSS

1. Ticket portion
5. List-ending abbr.
8. Cat's cry
12. Greek liqueur
13. A word of support
14. Queen Elizabeth II's daughter
15. Shipboard slammer
16. On the button
18. Follow as a result
20. Barkeep on "The Simpsons"
21. Lamb Chop, for one
27. Wager
30. Anti's vote
31. Birthday celebration
32. Like Goodwill goods
34. "_____ Love You" (Beatles hit)
36. Roll's partner
37. Amassed, as a bar bill
39. Holiday threshold
41. "_____ Believes in Me" (Kenny Rogers song)
42. Hole-cutting machine
45. Speed along
46. Mutt
50. Species of maple
55. Price of a cab ride
56. Works on a comic book
57. Movie for which Jamie Foxx won an Oscar
58. Interruption noise
59. Snoring letters?
60. It's all in vein
61. Drags to court

DOWN

1. Black Tea 3G maker
2. Revolve
3. Guns in an action flick
4. Phony
5. Triage centers: abbr.
6. Flat topper
7. Nickname for a boxer
8. Shoot well on the links
9. Final word
10. Put _____ show
11. Cleverly constructed trap
17. Sudden stroke
19. Very long time
22. Toy pistol ammo
23. Band leader Kay
24. Country-club employees
25. Engrave on metal

26. Au pair's charge
27. Tupperware closure noise
28. Jacob's twin brother
29. Ken. neighbor
33. Title for Camilla Parker Bowles
35. "_____ had it!"
38. Singer Collins
40. Unproven power: abbr.
43. Martinez with three Cy Young Awards

44. Living room furniture pieces
47. Its highest peak is Mount Ka'ala
48. Manitoba tribe
49. Bottom lines?
50. Show _____
51. Showstopper in "A Chorus Line"
52. Classic Jaguar
53. Cochlea's locale
54. Whiskey variety

19 | Jennifer Who?

ACROSS

1. Bubbly foam
5. Gets rid of confusion
13. Somewhat
14. Small cars
15. A singer/actress + a tennis player
17. Take a bite
18. Old Mario Bros. console
19. Place for pigs
20. "No Ordinary Love" singer
24. Active arcade game with arrows and a floor pad: abbr.
25. Words said after a challenge or dare
26. Suffix after concept or event
27. Oscar-winning singer/actress + an actress
30. Tarzan's friend
31. Emotional support-seeking
32. "This American Life" host Glass
33. Spice Girl Halliwell
34. "The Daily Show" host Stewart
37. Maidenform item
38. Maria Shriver, to John F. Kennedy
40. An actress + another actress
46. "That's totally correct!"
47. Oath for Dr. Watson
48. Beef that may be cubed before packaging
49. Without, in French

DOWN

1. Prepares pretzels
2. WWII German sub: hyph.
3. The green Teletubby
4. "Leave in," to a proofreader
5. 300, to Nero
6. Mauna _____ (Aloha State erupter)
7. King's equivalent: abbr.
8. Busy month for the IRS
9. Bollywood actress Aishwarya _____
10. Controversy in tabloids
11. Totally
12. Greek letters that look like tridents
16. Scrapes an orange peel

21. "With _____ in My Heart"
22. Alms recipient
23. Put in data
24. In the proper manner
25. Think tank output
27. Required wear for some food servers
28. Lift higher
29. Actress Menzel of "Wicked"
34. Game where things tend to fall apart

35. Arctic, for one
36. Sci-fi and comic book lovers, stereotypically
37. Howls at the moon
39. Bouts of anger
41. Opposite of NNE
42. Faith's country-singing husband
43. Smelted stuff
44. Grant-providing organization: abbr.
45. Apprehend

20 | Island Getaway

ACROSS

1. Frisbee, for one
5. In vogue
9. Insane
12. _____ ID (log-on need)
13. Indian musical term
14. Skater's surface
15. Islands visited by Darwin
17. Pencil end
18. Collar, as a criminal
19. South Seas home of Gauguin
21. Once more
24. Attack on all sides
25. Island off Mozambique where lemurs live
29. "Nova" airer
30. MGM's lion
31. Breeze provider
34. Island where you'll find San Juan
38. Norwegian playwright
41. Not drunk
42. U.S. state comprised of islands
44. _____ carte
45. Santa _____ winds

46. Greek vacation island
51. Moving-day rental
52. Actor Epps
53. Garden spot
54. Yellowstone grazer
55. California wine valley
56. Sunup

DOWN

1. Excavated
2. "Last one in _____ rotten egg!"
3. TV remote abbr.
4. Brain protectors: var.
5. Maryland seafood specialty
6. Witchy woman
7. Gershwin's "_____ Rhythm"
8. Winter melon
9. Short skirts
10. Like angles less than 90 degrees
11. "Credit or _____?"
16. Twinge
20. That girl
21. Rock concert blaster
22. Yak

23. Online pop-ups, often
26. Pub drink
27. Rev.'s speech
28. Removable bed
31. Little lie
32. Perfect tennis serve
33. _____ 'easter
34. Princess's mattress problem
35. A choir may sing in it
36. Norwegian capital
37. Howled like a lion

38. "_____ a dream": King
39. Hackneyed
40. Two-time Oscar winner Hilary
43. "_____ Rock" (Simon & Garfunkel hit)
44. Gillette razor
47. 40 winks
48. Actress Lupino
49. Modern
50. B&B

21 | Holiday Traditions

ACROSS

1. IV hooker-uppers
4. Location gizmo, for short
7. Latin music
12. Alley-_____ (basketball maneuver)
13. Golden yrs. cache
14. Fairy tale character
15. Rowing tool
16. Vote in Vichy
17. Swashbuckling Flynn
18. When we eat the big bird
21. Hearty swallow
22. Cherry or cranberry
23. When we give treats to children
26. Feel far from fine
29. Mineral deposits
30. Historic period
31. Isn't ungrammatical
32. Signaled "thumbs up"
33. When we party before Lent
35. Mr. Potato Head stick-on
36. Trickle through the cracks
37. When we give gifts to loved ones
42. Oversized
43. Adam's donation
44. Carrier to Tokyo, quickly
45. Bello of "The Cooler"
46. Blackjack necessity
47. Artist Maya
48. Oscar winner Marisa
49. Bosom buddy
50. Heart exam: abbr.

DOWN

1. Cheer (for)
2. Genesis animal shelter
3. Spread out
4. Source of fan-shaped leaves
5. Old hands
6. Crooned a tune
7. Filmmaker Spielberg
8. Roll-on brand
9. Lonely, often coupled with "love"
10. Toil wearily
11. Best effort
19. Zeros
20. "_____ you loud and clear"

23. Owl's cry
24. Becomes frayed
25. Make a blunder
26. Terrier type
27. Hysterical
28. Capt. saluters
31. Many a moon
33. Rum cocktail
34. Sanford of "The Jeffersons"
35. Bert's "Sesame Street" pal
37. "See you later"
38. Do damage to
39. Mouth, slangily
40. Flaky rock
41. Cristina _____ ("Grey's Anatomy" doctor)
42. UK clock setting

EASY

ACROSS

1. Bakery purchase
4. Cockeyed
9. Affirmation at the altar
12. Personals
13. Fred Flintstone's boss
14. Cotillion star
15. LaPaglia crime drama
18. Grove fruit
19. Outbursts of revelation
20. Chihuahua or California
21. Flatter
23. Little goat
24. The great Garbo
26. Reply to an implied insult
32. Cars
33. Cloister member
34. When Romeo met Juliet
37. Holding a grudge against
39. Impulse
40. Eugene's place
42. Decorating knack, say
46. Get something out of
47. Tony winner Worth
48. Spelling competition
49. Foreign Inc.
50. Goes on and on
51. NFL scores

DOWN

1. Fido's foot
2. Extremely stupid
3. "CHiPs" costar Erik
4. Conjointly
5. Counterfeit coin
6. Beckinsale of "Underworld"
7. Airport schedule abbr.
8. Soaked
9. Washington neighbor
10. Sticker of a sort
11. Fat
16. Panama or porkpie
17. Bangalore biggie
20. Downhill runner
21. Catastrophic endings?
22. Tell _____ glance
24. Tollbooth barrier
25. "Bringing Up Baby" studio
27. Wynonna's ma

28. Wine vessel
29. Uncertain
30. Skillfully subtle
31. Explosive stick: abbr.
34. Worth zero stars
35. Where VapoRub may be rubbed
36. Like track-and-field races

37. Passes out
38. Past
40. Change, sometimes
41. 1996 winner of both the Pulitzer and the Tony
43. Zip
44. Certain S&L account
45. Gents

EASY

ACROSS

1. Grind into pulp
5. Boxer's target
8. Small dog breed
12. Hotel room posting
13. Grand _____ Opry
14. Verbal
15. Draped outfit of India
16. Sounds from an infant
18. Solemn vow
20. Lisper's bane
21. Casserole container
26. "Right you _____!"
27. "_____ go bragh"
28. Pay heed to
32. Insulting comment
34. Three _____ match
35. Scheherazade offering
36. Crosby's "Road" pictures costar
37. In good health
39. Celtics' and Clippers' org.
40. Old West fighter
43. Ball's husband
46. "Raven" maniac?
47. Drive-in menu selection
51. Unemployed
54. Author Morrison
55. Keogh alternative
56. What farmers till
57. Not on land
58. Hair goo
59. Concludes

DOWN

1. "_____ Doubtfire"
2. Bond rating
3. Begin, as a conversation
4. Supermodel Klum
5. Employment
6. Fla. neighbor
7. Network
8. Bit of criticism
9. Pitchers' stats, for short
10. Curly cabbage
11. Service organization
17. "Exactly right!"
19. Less than two
21. Heavy blow
22. Folkie Guthrie
23. Matured

24. Attends a banquet
25. Combined
29. Struck loudly
30. Hamburg's river
31. Calendar span
33. Cape and tiara, e.g.
38. Word before service or reading
41. Submachine gun
42. Loud sound

43. Former Nationals and Indians manager Manny
44. Density symbols
45. Striped yellow ball in pool
48. Use a shovel
49. Tram load
50. Guy's partner
52. Pan cover
53. Alligators have a couple

24 | Out of Brooklyn

ACROSS
1. Complete and utter
6. Place to hang your coat
9. Slap on
12. Gerald's predecessor
13. Torch lighter at the 1996 Olympics
14. Fifth word of "The Star-Spangled Banner"
15. Latin father
16. President born in 1908: inits.
17. Yours may be picked up, if you're lucky
18. Domestic sitcom, with "The"
21. _____ mode
22. Dress in
23. Beta beater
26. Yellowstone herd member
28. Royal address
31. Star of 18-Across
35. _____ gin fizz
36. Non-smoking ordinance, e.g.
37. "Here's looking at you, _____"
38. Spritzes

41. Actress Thompson of "Back to the Future"
43. Role played by 31-Across
48. Yves's yes
49. Wish otherwise
50. Drive
52. Fancy planter
53. Word before school or Vic
54. Farm song refrain
55. Game of pursuit
56. Golfer Ernie
57. Surgical aid

DOWN
1. Sugar serving: abbr.
2. Brightly colored fish
3. Yugoslavian leader, once
4. Battle locale
5. "Gentlemen Prefer Blondes" girl
6. Conceal in the hand
7. Nudge with a joint
8. Action figure
9. Mark on Roger Maris's record?
10. Cherished
11. Belles of the balls

19. School in New Haven
20. Atlantis launchers: abbr.
23. Music channel hosts, for short
24. Rogue computer in "2001: A Space Odyssey"
25. Looking grumpy
27. CIA rival, once
29. Ruler, in Rouen
30. Football position
32. Hold on to

33. Refrain syllables
34. Foes
39. Paroxysm
40. Head of the anatomy class?
42. Come clean about
43. Runaway victory
44. Enveloping glow
45. Cincinnati team
46. Certain sword
47. Rheinland refusal
51. Sodom refugee

25 | Wok-aholic

ACROSS

1. He had a whale of a tale
6. Lawyers' org.
9. "Isn't _____ Lovely" (1976 Wonder tune)
12. Voice a view
13. "_____ Misérables"
14. Mystery writer Stout
15. Szechuan dish
18. Biblical birthright seller
19. Visualize
20. "The Sun _____ Rises"
21. Irritate
23. "Giant" author Ferber
25. Humiliate
28. Andean tuber
29. "The Matrix" lead role
32. Chinese-American dish
35. Faucet
36. Command to Fido
37. Oil-yielding rock
38. Angered
40. "Bill _____ the Science Guy"
41. Gumbo veggie
43. "Dig in!"
45. Poisonous snakes
49. Chinese dish
52. "Jamaica _____" (1939 Hitchcock film)
53. Gidget portrayer Sandra
54. Skin layer
55. Dress (up)
56. Perform basic arithmetic
57. Laundry appliance

DOWN

1. Roast ingredient?
2. Numbered work
3. Singer Simone
4. Distress
5. In the know
6. Lotion base
7. Pray
8. "Evil Dead" hero
9. Ceylon today
10. Does a tailor's job
11. '67 Montreal event
16. Billy Joel's "Don't _____ Me Why"
17. Kurosawa classic
22. Actress Witherspoon
24. Flower in a chain

25. Take the stage
26. A sheep remark
27. Hoping (to)
28. Mo. with United Nations Day
30. Anago, in Japanese cuisine
31. With 48-Down, poor movie rating
33. Let out, as a garment
34. Crook

39. British rule in India
40. High degree
41. Note in passing?
42. Numbers game
44. Like fine wine
46. Vigorous
47. Fleshy fruit
48. See 31-Down
50. Nev. neighbor
51. "The _____ Couple"

26 | Don't Fail Me Now!

ACROSS

1. Make the grade?
5. Criticize, slangily
8. Q-tip
12. Break in the action
13. Strike caller, for short
14. Lot of loot
15. Mozart's "Madamina," e.g.
16. Second degree?: abbr.
17. Priestly garb
18. Pack (down)
19. Clunker
20. "Can't Help Lovin' _____ Man"
21. Window cleaner's tool
25. Nile biter
28. Speaker's hesitations
29. Synthetic silk
32. Sunglasses, familiarly
34. Tranquil
35. French military hats
36. Everyday article
37. Morning moisture
38. Petitions
41. In accordance with
43. "Yikes!"
44. "_____ for the poor"
48. Steams
50. _____ Beta Kappa
51. In _____ of (replacing)
52. Grimm beast
53. "_____ the land of the free…"
54. "Immediately!": abbr.
55. It smells
56. Darjeeling or oolong
57. June honorees

DOWN

1. Surveyor's map
2. Certain something
3. _____ Jim (beef jerky brand)
4. High-fives
5. Lollipops made by Spangler Candy Company
6. Pervades
7. Comic David of TV's "Rules of Engagement"
8. Masseur's workplace, maybe
9. Deranged-looking
10. Jessica of "Dark Angel"
11. Numero uno
22. Mission

23. Roll out the red carpet for
24. Ring bearer, maybe
25. "Don't _____!"
26. Cow or sow
27. Those who work on walls
30. Bit of binary code
31. "What's _____ with you?"
33. Cacophony
34. "Hips Don't Lie" singer
36. [Giggle]
39. Move, as a plant
40. Leaves for lunch?
41. Subatomic particle
42. Descartes's "therefore"
45. "The Simpsons" character who is good at crossword puzzles
46. Honeyed drink
47. Dines
49. "Didn't I tell you?"

27 | Profits in Baskets

ACROSS

1. Carpenter's holder
5. Satellite receiver
9. Chew the fat
12. Publisher Adolph
13. Black-and-white sandwich
14. A, in Arles
15. Unconscious state
17. Neither Rep. nor Dem.
18. Abduct
19. More malicious
21. T or F, on exams
22. Playground cry
24. _____ noire
25. "The Wizard _____" (comic strip)
26. Irish poet and playwright
27. All profit, in the NBA?
31. _____ a time
32. Swiss mountains
33. Atlanta Brave, for one
34. Get ready
35. No-goodnik
38. Upper house
40. Danny of "Do the Right Thing"
42. Chiang _____-shek
43. Gift from a bunny
45. Direct ending
46. Land measure
47. Sir's counterpart
48. The, in Berlin
49. Tim of "WKRP in Cincinnati"
50. It can be figured in square feet

DOWN

1. Screwdriver ingredient
2. Cause winter isolation for
3. Takes off
4. Armchair athlete's channel
5. Miami athlete
6. Rage
7. Terse summons
8. Show optimism
9. Certain African
10. Bening of "American Beauty"

11. Treatment for many illnesses
16. Deemed appropriate
20. Helps during the heist
23. Mystery writers' award
25. Mitchell's Scarlett
26. Modern affluent type
27. Like studded tires
28. Enjoying a furlough
29. More minute
30. Sounded like a lamb
34. Type of sign or pipe
35. Like crystal
36. Simple plants
37. Accepted doctrine
39. Pull apart
41. Humorist Bombeck
44. Hindu title

28 | Football's Famous Brothers

ACROSS

1. Apple computers
5. Call's partner
9. Compass pt.
12. "I smell _____!"
13. "Little" girl of comic books
14. _____ whim
15. A few
16. Saudi, usually
17. Not taut
18. Designation both Peyton and Eli have received
21. Stage whisper
22. Iowa State's town
23. Prefix with thermal
24. Peyton and Eli's dad, himself a football star
28. Poet _____ St. Vincent Millay
30. College e-mail ending
31. Haughty one
35. Peyton and Eli make a lot of them
38. Eggs in labs
39. Make this at a track
41. Walked nervously

43. College honor bestowed upon both Peyton and Eli
47. Peyton and Eli, position-wise: abbr.
48. Margarine
49. Opposed to
50. "A mouse!"
51. Jewelry for Peyton or Eli after winning the big game
52. Run in neutral
53. Medics: abbr.
54. Actress Winslet
55. Playthings

DOWN

1. Rolfing, for example
2. Stirred up
3. "The Piano" director Jane
4. War horse
5. Tattle
6. Widespread currency
7. Lobster's pincer
8. Grandson of Genghis Khan
9. Tackle a crossword

10. Peyton and Eli take a lot of them
11. Floor coat
19. Stephen of "The Crying Game"
20. Married Fr. women
25. Hi-_____ monitor
26. LP successors
27. Color shade
29. Summit
32. Quitter's phrase
33. In an open manner
34. Good guys' foes
36. In the office
37. Hot tub
39. Color of honey
40. Soaks in the sun
42. Stand by for
44. Director Kazan
45. Pre-Easter time
46. Theater section
47. Proof-ending abbr.

29 | Relax!

ACROSS

1. Globe
4. Apt name for a Dalmatian
8. SNL act
12. Bettor's letters
13. Like Liberace's hair
14. Long-bodied fish
15. Relax!
17. Frozen desserts
18. Do a salon job
19. African mongoose
21. "_____ a Wonderful Life"
23. Chesapeake Bay catch
24. Treaty
27. It was once Siam
31. Grp. advocating tooth care
32. Obliterate
33. Not pro
34. Most fusty
36. Gumbo vegetable
37. Bog
38. Maple tree fluid
40. Gizmos
43. "Key _____" (Bogart classic)
47. Burn soother
48. Relax!
50. "Broadcast _____" (William Hurt film)
51. Top-notch
52. "Jeopardy!" host Fleming
53. Lady's man
54. Optimistic
55. Pair

DOWN

1. Art supplies
2. Cheer (for)
3. Channel marker
4. Amiable
5. Cookware item
6. Egg cell
7. Puts in an expected role
8. Nautilus shell shape
9. Relax!
10. Furniture retailer
11. Examination
16. Skirt opening
20. One of the Great Lakes
22. Vehicle for Blanche DuBois

24. Actress Dawber
25. Hubbub
26. Relax!
28. Owns
29. Neither companion
30. "CSI" evidence
32. Ireland, to the Irish
35. Abridged work
36. Milky gemstone
39. Bowling lane

40. "West Side Story" faction
41. Away from the wind
42. "Bug off!"
44. Caldwell's "Tobacco _____"
45. Ashram figure
46. Kevin in "A Fish Called Wanda"
49. Current officeholders

EASY

ACROSS

1. Decorating ribbon
6. "Boardwalk Empire" network
9. Scratch
12. Off the ground
13. Sick
14. Memorable time period
15. Santa's reindeer, e.g.
16. Biblical he-man
18. Dog restraint
20. Sign of a sellout: abbr.
21. Join forces (with)
25. iPhone download, for short
28. Flightless bird
30. Eroded
31. Yellow dairy product
35. Spider's cousin
36. Privy
37. Person used by others
38. Votes in
41. Two make a quart: abbr.
43. Original anchor of "Weekend Update" on "Saturday Night Live"
48. Capital city of 9.5 million

51. It comes straight from the heart
52. Tuna at a sushi bar
53. Little green men: abbr.
54. Wrinkly greens
55. Pile of green
56. "_____ is me"
57. Wed in haste

DOWN

1. Colorful foam shoe, familiarly
2. Country music duo Big & _____
3. Regarding, on memos
4. Sneaks a look
5. Keyed in
6. Way up there
7. Distend
8. Stan's friend, in old comedies
9. _____ culpa
10. Painting or photography
11. "Yay, team!"
17. At a loss for words, maybe
19. State of deep unconsciousness

22. Tavern in Springfield
23. _____ Minor (constellation)
24. Chick's chirp
25. Pinnacle
26. TV host Donahue
27. Townshend of The Who
29. Website ID
32. British record label established in 1929
33. Cheat on a test, in a way

34. Food in a stack
39. Pitched
40. Donnybrook: hyph.
42. Sandbar
44. Ming Dynasty collectible
45. Janis's comics partner
46. Numbered instruction
47. Stress-free living
48. Talk, talk, talk
49. "Now I get it"
50. Farm youngster

31 | Toot Toot

ACROSS

1. Mild cigar
6. "I knew it!"
9. Plumb on "The Brady Bunch"
12. Baltimore footballer
13. Guitar pioneer Paul
14. Permit
15. Occurrence
16. General Grant, to his friends
18. Old-fashioned hearing aid
20. Knight's title
21. Place to keep a horse
25. Phrase before carte or king
28. "Four score and seven years _____ ..."
30. Superhero's attire
31. Site of Custer's Last Stand
35. Physics or data preceder
36. Prelude to matrimony
37. Vote for
38. Traffic troubles
41. Familiar place for a cat
43. Peter Parker's newspaper in "Spider-Man"
48. West Indies musical style
51. Popular sandwich cookies
52. Keats' "On Melancholy," e.g.
53. Letter on Clark Kent's chest
54. Empty the container
55. Wet, spongy ground
56. It's used in saponification
57. Ill-tempered

DOWN

1. First Nations tribe of Manitoba
2. Proctor & Gamble soap
3. State surely
4. Common budget items
5. Being judged
6. Reunion attendee, briefly
7. Pitches in
8. Up to the present
9. High rails: abbr.

10. Shape formed by geese in flight
11. UFO flyers
17. Treasure trove
19. Basic impulse
22. Sealane marker
23. Former Milan money
24. Italian volcano
25. Charitable donations
26. Claim on a property
27. "_____ boy!"
29. "The Mikado" accessory
32. Belated

33. A way to stand by
34. Proceed
39. Campaign-button spot
40. Spacek of "Carrie"
42. Race stakes
44. Be the "also-ran"
45. Thousands, in slang
46. Yahoo
47. Catch sight of
48. Kernel holder
49. Commotion
50. Advantage, with "up"

32 | Triple Jump

ACROSS

1. PC connectors
5. Part of Latin conjugation practice
9. Maxim
12. Like-minded voters
13. Mine find
14. More than vexation
15. Boo-bird's call
16. Gathering dust
17. End of a series
18. Green Bay Packer's celebration
21. Green vegetable
22. Financial page highlight: abbr.
23. Flying expert
26. Kabuki costume belt
28. Powwow
32. Simon and Garfunkel song
36. Confident to an extreme
37. Korean carmaker
38. Canine examiner's degree: abbr.
39. VW hatchback
42. Cry at a bullfight
44. Soap brand
49. Actor Cruise
50. Raines or Grasso
51. "Veni, vidi, _____"
54. Book reviewer?: abbr.
55. Address for a lady
56. "The Good Earth" wife
57. Whammy
58. "¿Cómo _____ usted?"
59. Jerk

DOWN

1. Great Society initials
2. Pub drink
3. Playwright Coward
4. Leftover
5. "Open sesame!" memorizer
6. Math class calculation
7. Dwight's opponent in '52 and '56
8. Start a hole
9. Mini or jumbo, e.g.
10. Geometric extent
11. Cry
19. Cat's cry
20. In _____ parentis (legal doctrine)

23. Sounds heard at physicals
24. Relative of .edu
25. Australian bird
27. Rile
29. 1963 Paul Newman film
30. "Body _____ Soul" (1947 movie)
31. Six-point plays: abbr.
33. Coddled items
34. Historical display
35. Indonesian island

40. The main idea
41. They are surrounded by agua
43. Ambassador's inferior
44. Athlete's foot symptom
45. Ring surrounder
46. Format for tall tales?
47. City map
48. _____ monster
52. Coffee container
53. Sign, as a deal

33 | Where Is She?

ACROSS

1. Mimicked
5. "Certainly!"
8. Senior citizen's advocacy org.
12. Took the train
13. Acorn dropper
14. June 6, 1944
15. The Show-Me State
17. Kuwaiti leader
18. Miscalculate
19. Backbone
20. Mother: Spanish
23. Achievements
25. Touched ground
26. Hoedown participants
27. Kindergarten or college: abbr.
30. "_____ a bird..."
31. Out of whack... or what's hiding in each theme entry
32. One of the Gershwins
33. "Mr. _____"
34. Dr. Zhivago's love
35. Webster of words
36. Lendl and Reitman
38. Salon tint
39. Foundation
41. Of recent origin
42. "If all _____ fails..."
43. Close call
48. Lion's greeting
49. Lofty mountain
50. Diva's number
51. Salon goops
52. Pizza buy
53. Notorious fiddler

DOWN

1. Militarize
2. Luau dish
3. Actors Harris and Asner
4. Desolate place
5. Part of MYOB
6. Organ of balance
7. Go downhill fast
8. Very skilled
9. Confession
10. Drops from the sky
11. Pile of combustibles
16. Mining product
19. Lippiness
20. Wound seriously
21. Singing voice

22. It precedes after-school pickup
23. Carnivals
24. Joy Adamson's lioness
26. FBI agent
28. Fruity prefix used by Ocean Spray
29. "LOL," in person
31. Lamenter's comment
35. Woodward's blue-eyed husband

37. Contenders
38. The Beatles' "I Saw _____ Standing There"
39. Ice float
40. Sunburn soother
41. Scruff
43. Tot's refresher
44. Yale booster
45. Land opener?
46. Elton John's title
47. _____ Paulo, Brazil

ACROSS

1. Watch pocket
4. Likely
7. _____ point (center of activity)
12. Eisenhower's nickname
13. Caviar, e.g.
14. Black
15. Writer Sue of the Kinsey Millhone alphabet mysteries
17. Greene of "Bonanza"
18. H. H. Munro's nom de plume
19. Arrive at the curb
21. In that place
23. Thwack a fly
26. Dell alternative
29. Genesis garden
30. Actress Garr
31. Actor Hawke
33. Singer K. T. _____
34. Ripped
35. Razor choice
38. Set down
39. Heroic tale
40. Egyptian capital
42. "Button your lip!"
44. Page
48. Preminger and Kruger
50. Writer Ruth whose "A Dark-Adapted Eye" won the '87 Edgar
52. Gullible
53. "Born in the _____"
54. Herbert Hoover's First Lady
55. Complies
56. Farm enclosure
57. Perceive

DOWN

1. Newton fruits
2. Southern veggie
3. Bird's bill
4. MoMA display
5. All tuckered out
6. Secure faculty status
7. Plummeted
8. Certain woodwind musicians
9. Crime novelist Patricia who writes the Dr. Kay Scarpetta series
10. Legendary advice columnist Landers
11. Soap ingredient
16. Temper tantrum

20. Ex-QB Dawson
22. Fowl female
24. Diva's song
25. Itsy-bitsy
26. Dole (out)
27. On the crest of
28. Author Agatha who
    created Hercule Poirot
    and Jane Marple
32. Pizza tidbit
33. Galley propeller
35. Behave

36. Zodiac sign in May
37. Most fully matured
41. On its last legs
43. Brings into play
45. Squirmy catches
46. Burn soother
47. Ventilation duct
48. "Double Fantasy" singer
49. Diet cola introduced in
    1963
51. Negative vote

35 | Ain't It Grand?

ACROSS

1. Pear variety
5. "Thunderstruck" band
9. Cook in fat
12. IHOP part: abbr.
13. Perlman of "Cheers"
14. "Would I _____ to You?" (Eurythmics tune)
15. Gumbo ingredient
16. "We Are _____" (2006 McConaughey movie)
18. "No Air" singer Jordin
20. Drive ahead
21. Aunt, in Mexico
22. Camera attachment
24. Grand _____
27. Geisha's sash
30. Sluggish
31. The Very Old Ewe in "Babe"
32. Untidy one
33. Coquettish
34. Grand _____
36. Supermodel Kate
37. Word after swimming or thinking
38. Legally prevent
41. Hawkeye State residents
44. Grand _____
47. Singer Clapton
48. Ad _____ committee
49. "Return of the Jedi" critter
50. Europe's most active volcano
51. "I'm impressed!"
52. Down Under jumpers, briefly
53. Twosome

DOWN

1. Book jacket briefs
2. Like a punished G.I., perhaps
3. Grand _____
4. Remove impurities from
5. Gives a gun to
6. When repeated, a Latin dance
7. "_____ Spiegel"
8. Caesars Palace, for one
9. Kind of bag
10. Madden
11. Use an outdoor voice

17. Letters in British ocean liner names
19. _____ Von D of "LA Ink"
22. Tropical feasts
23. Latin "and others"
24. "Cake Boss" network
25. "Yoo-_____!"
26. Singer Tori
27. Grand _____
28. Feathery scarf
29. Apple competitor
32. Type of wrap
34. Penny metal

35. "The Name of the Rose" author Umberto
36. Matriarch, casually
38. Repeat after me?
39. Chase off
40. RPM measurer
41. Signs, as a check
42. "Project Runway" judge Garcia
43. Multitude
45. _____ Jima
46. Tic-tac-toe win

36 | Gene Kelly

ACROSS

1. Bachelor's place
4. Genetic letters
7. Anjou or Bartlett
11. _____-Wan Kenobi
12. China neighbor
13. Son of Woody
14. "_____ Girls" (1957 Kelly film)
15. Freeze front?
16. "The Happy _____" (1957 Kelly film)
17. Kelly's partner in "Singin' in the Rain"
20. Wife or husband
22. "_____ sad but true"
23. Astringent stuff
24. [As written]
25. Water cooler
28. Kelly's costar in "Singin' in the Rain"
32. Likely to catch on quickly
33. ISP with a circle-in-a-triangle logo
34. "My Name Is _____" (TV series)
35. 60 secs.
36. Novelist Charlotte

38. Kelly's partner in "Summer Stock"
42. Cut _____
43. Clunker
44. "On _____ Little Houseboat" (Kelly duet with Shirley MacLaine)
47. Notion
48. Duplex or studio
49. Ryder Cup team
50. Temporary pause
51. Keatsian "always"
52. Pro _____ (for now)

DOWN

1. Washington type
2. Maggie Simpson's grandpa
3. Reduce in price
4. Emulate Kelly
5. Portrayer of Mr. Big on "Sex and the City"
6. Eastern
7. "An American in _____" (1951 Kelly musical)
8. Arrow shooter of myth
9. Alack's partner
10. Needled
12. Boys

18. "3:10 to _____"
19. "Little Caesar" nickname
20. Tony winner Thompson
21. Fall heavily
24. The Sun
25. Quick shopping stop
26. Bud of "Brewster McCloud"
27. First name in legal fiction
29. "Mare's _____" (gun on "Wanted: Dead or Alive")
30. Talk show giant Phil
31. Broadway light gas

35. "For Me and _____" (Kelly's first movie)
36. Betsy _____, Kelly's first wife
37. Mesmerized
38. Hoosegow
39. Language written in Persian-Arabic letters
40. Fight with Kelly in "The Three Musketeers"
41. French director Clair
45. Customary practice
46. Ewe mate

37 | Bea Plus

ACROSS

1. Madison's state: abbr.
5. Johnny who plays Jack Sparrow
9. Paramedic of sorts: abbr.
12. Tan shade
13. "A miss _____ good as a mile"
14. Losing tic-tac-toe line
15. Dancer Gene's ursine cousin?
17. "True Blood" network
18. Hospital unit
19. 2008 Obama opponent
21. "The Hulk" director Lee
24. U.S. set of freeways
26. Drags
27. Just enough food to feed baby chicks?
30. Remedy
31. Groove
32. Pathologist's suffix
35. Power cell that fits on a necklace?
38. Play for time
40. Mick Jagger title
41. _____ Moines, Iowa
42. Adenoid neighbor
44. Badminton divider

46. Cartoonist Chast
47. Top worn by a drummer?
52. Prefix before "scope"
53. Tabloid twosome
54. Microscopic bit
55. Submissions to publishers: abbr.
56. Slightly mad
57. "Mickey" singer Basil

DOWN

1. Charlotte's craft
2. Rocks, in a bar
3. Mrs., in Madrid
4. "_____ Your Enthusiasm"
5. Went with a fight, like old habits
6. Course for new citizens: abbr.
7. Frond-ly plant?
8. "We all go a little mad sometimes" movie
9. Completely wiped out
10. Oil company that merged with Exxon
11. Saturday morning fare, slangily
16. Actor Dullea of "2001: A Space Odyssey"

20. "Quiet, you!"
21. "The Bachelor" network
22. New, in Nuremburg
23. Beans in a three-bean salad, usually
25. Ticket leftovers
28. Passes out, with "over"
29. Refrain from Creedence Clearwater Revival's "Fortunate Son"
33. Burning anger
34. Part of CBS: abbr.
36. Excuses in court

37. Low numero
38. Late senator Thurmond
39. Hits the car horn
43. Actor Jared whose band is 30 Seconds to Mars
45. "_____ '70s Show"
48. _____ Lingus (Irish airline)
49. Lance of the O.J. Trial
50. Harry and Hermione's friend
51. "Wow, I didn't need to know that" inits.

38 | Canine Anagrams

ACROSS

1. Thaw
5. Sundance offering
9. "Uncle Tom's Cabin" heroine
12. Charles Lamb's pen name
13. Janis's comics companion
14. Off the shelf
15. DIANA MALT
17. Salon stiffener
18. Key above Shift
19. Scurrilous attack
21. Classified info?
22. NEAT EDGAR
26. Harts' mates
27. Walkie-talkie word
28. Numeral next to plus sign
31. More than a job
33. Average
34. Subject of the book "Bush's Brain"
35. PINK GEESE
38. Oral hygiene grp.
41. Gerald Ford's birthplace
42. Barbershop blade
44. Protrude
46. DAD'S HUNCH
48. Aristotle's H
49. Sondheim's "_____ the Woods"
50. Florentine river
51. Noted Downing Street address
52. Farrier's file
53. Wall Street pessimist

DOWN

1. Sorceress of Greek myth
2. Large antelope
3. Sings rhythmically
4. Domesticate
5. Blubber
6. Eye parts
7. Andean pack animal
8. "Haystacks" artist
9. Inscribe
10. Sign from Churchill
11. Hole puncher
16. Inert gas used in lasers
20. Worship

23. Hammett novel "_____ Harvest" (1929)
24. Maiden name indicator
25. Blunder
26. Levi's fabric
28. Roadie's haul
29. Barely passable grade
30. Upper Midwesterner
31. Fortune 500 members: abbr.
32. Maintains

34. Responds to a stimulus
36. Low point
37. West African nation
38. Light blue
39. Actress Reed
40. Passion
43. Captain of the Pequod
44. Fast plane
45. Beehive State native
47. Bygone school dance

39 | First Ladies First

ACROSS

1. Lowlife
5. Opposite of masc.
8. Hemingway's "For _____ the Bell Tolls"
12. "_____ you don't!"
13. The "tan" in a "black and tan"
14. Sleek, for short
15. First first lady to visit an overseas combat zone
18. Christian minister
19. "Sesame Street" viewer
20. "Le smoking" pioneer's monogram
21. First first lady to hold a college degree
26. Brand, in a way
27. "Dreams from My Father" author
28. Blowgun ammo
31. Certain digital watch face, for short
33. "It's my turn to bat!"
34. "La Bohème," e.g.
36. Cold cuts, e.g.
38. First first lady to write a commercially published book

40. Baseball's rule enforcer: abbr.
43. Dined
44. Hang around
46. First first lady to win an Emmy
50. Bridge toll unit
51. Nervous trait
52. Beethoven's "Archduke _____"
53. Garden intruder
54. Pillbox, e.g.
55. Fly high

DOWN

1. Mawkish
2. Barbecues badly
3. Up to the time when
4. "Encore!"
5. Real
6. Denzel Washington's "The Book of _____"
7. Substantial
8. "Be patient"
9. Bewitch
10. "_____ y Plata" (Montana's motto)
11. Back-to-work day: abbr.
16. Archipelago part

17. Area west of the Bowery
22. Caffè additive
23. Starchy tuber
24. Australian runner
25. Plant fluid
26. Ran nude
28. "Stupid me!"
29. "Tarzan" mimic
30. Bill of Rights subj.
32. Parry
35. Against
37. "This thing weighs ____!"
39. Choppers, so to speak
40. In ____ (not yet born)
41. TV, radio, etc.
42. Comedian Richard
45. QB turnovers
46. Big part of a dinosaur skeleton
47. Can
48. Diminutive suffix
49. Sedona maker

MEDIUM

ACROSS

1. Handheld computer: abbr.
4. Stock option
8. R&B singer Redding
12. German link
13. Plant with spiny-edged leaves
14. 2005 musical with Taye Diggs
15. Where Columbia University moved to in 1857
18. Say over
19. Ancient Athenian assembly area
20. Turns over
21. Looked daggers (at)
22. Rough figure: abbr.
23. Squelched
25. Erskine Caldwell novel featuring Jeeter Lester
30. Bumblers
31. Father figures
33. "Private Lives" playwright Noël
36. Baseball brother Bret or Aaron
38. Disjointedly
39. Platypuses do it
41. Site of many fashion boutiques
43. Shade provider
44. Front money
45. Prior to, in verse
46. Bitsy preceder
47. Line of symmetry
48. Fast jet: abbr.

DOWN

1. Stone used by pedicurists
2. "CSI" procedure
3. Put in, as ingredients
4. Spanish houses
5. What little things mean, in song
6. Kind of wolf
7. Perrins's partner
8. Ristorante herb
9. Opera voice
10. Get used (to)
11. Lieu

Crossword grid with numbered cells: 1, 2, 3, 4, 5, 6, 7, 8, 9, 10, 11 (top row); 12, 13, 14; 15, 16, 17; 18, 19; 20, 21; 22, 23, 24; 25, 26, 27, 28, 29; 30, 31, 32; 33, 34, 35, 36, 37; 38, 39, 40; 41, 42; 43, 44, 45; 46, 47, 48.

16. Feeling of rage
17. Courage under fire
21. Pontiac muscle cars
23. Missile in 1990s news
24. Pretense
26. Nonsense
27. Vital carrier
28. Orbital extremes
29. Risks
32. Italian sonnet's end
33. Plants in a dry place
34. Abstract visual images
35. Articles of merchandise
36. Computer capacity
37. Contraction in "The Star-Spangled Banner"
39. Minnesota's WNBA team
40. Italian city known for sparkling wines
42. Sheep's sound

41 | Nobody's Spouse

ACROSS

1. Tend to the sauce
5. Math subject: abbr.
9. Marcher's syllable
12. Racer Yarborough
13. Fine-tune
14. "Before" of old
15. Party with no guest list
17. FBI guy
18. Painting or sculpture, e.g.
19. Lucky number
21. Lets loose
22. Singer Brewer
23. Kind of stick
26. First name in footwear
27. Husband or wife?
32. "_____ off?"
33. Pacific repast
34. Steamy places
36. Smart remark
41. Actor Flynn
42. Relax
44. Singer/actor Bon Jovi
45. Story that might include a dragon
47. "Hurrah, José!"
48. Goofing off
49. "I cannot tell _____"
50. Global traveler Nellie
51. Snaky swimmers
52. Word before hand or rags

DOWN

1. Jeer
2. Endangered species with a long snout
3. Actress Graff
4. "Cold Mountain" star Zellweger
5. Norse thunder god
6. Defeat decisively
7. Elected officials
8. V formation fliers
9. Forcible ejection
10. Incites
11. Honeybun, for example
16. Door fasteners
20. One-named designer
22. Cicero's garment
24. Protects against rust

25. African antelope
27. Rhinoplasty, familiarly
28. In the zone
29. Sporting contest
30. Florence's river
31. Like a rabbit's foot, supposedly
35. Title role for Jude or Michael

37. Label differently
38. In the least
39. Salsa singer Cruz
40. Jabbed with a joint
42. Pull a plow
43. Hawkish deity
46. Fruit-drink suffix

42 | Court Order

ACROSS

1. Small indentation
5. Expression of disapproval
8. Hammering sounds
12. February forecast
13. Polloi preceder
14. DSL subscriber
15. Gather with difficulty
17. John Glenn's state
18. Court figure
20. Counterpart to omega
21. Treasury division: abbr.
22. Gumbo veggie
25. Very old: abbr.
26. Color shade
29. Court figure
33. "Sprechen _____ Deutsch?"
34. _____ Kipper
35. Bridges of electricity
36. Lettered sandwich
37. Area between outfielders
39. Court figure
45. Last year's senior, for short
46. One not in the in group
47. Brush partner
48. Clip-_____ (certain sunglasses)
49. Western Colorado feature
50. Word-processing mistake
51. Bop-It, e.g.
52. Bolts down

DOWN

1. Furtive summons
2. First word of fairy tales
3. Foot trouble
4. African heritage festival
5. What we have here
6. Starting fare, often
7. Mowgli's creator Rudyard
8. Keeps afloat
9. Big Apple stadium
10. Rabin's predecessor
11. Box office sign: abbr.
16. Bakery purchase
19. Keystone site
22. Sterile places: abbr.
23. Japanese carp

24. Bread choice
25. Objective
26. "Death Becomes
    _____" (1992 Meryl
    Streep movie)
27. Trojan initials
28. Sink trap's shape
30. Hunky actor Waggoner
31. Skedaddles, with "it"
32. Midday break for
    toddlers

36. Hardly an intellectual
37. Bold
38. Yahoo
39. Overwhelm with
    sweetness
40. Something to get over
41. 2007 Ellen Page movie
42. It's all in your head
43. "_____ la guerre"
44. Memorable time periods
45. Vaudeville bit

43 | Get a Hold of Me

ACROSS

1. "One Tree Hill" star _____ Michael Murray
5. Dove's cry
8. Support system?
11. Wiggly dance
12. Home of the "You've Got Mail" guy
13. The Road Runner's legs, often
14. Teen-_____
15. "Sesame Street" character
17. Short dispatch on a 40-Across
19. Grab (all the blankets)
20. Lake near Nevada
23. Part of PBS: abbr.
26. Maya Angelou, e.g.
29. Struck a bell
30. Communication form fading due to 17-Across and 40-Across
33. Butter alternative
34. "I understand"
35. Kanga's son, in "Winnie the Pooh"
36. _____ del Rey (Los Angeles community)

38. Uno plus uno
40. It's used to make calls while out
46. Have an icky flavor
48. State with confirmation
49. Gulf of Mexico contents: Span.
50. Pharmaceutical company _____ Lilly
51. Michael of "Arrested Development"
52. Britney Spears genre
53. What some spray-ons replicate
54. Shoelace snarl

DOWN

1. IM conversation
2. Gigantic
3. Quiz show smartie Trebek
4. _____ Vader
5. Quiz show selection
6. _____ and aahs
7. Bullfight cheers
8. Marge Simpson feature
9. Get out fast
10. Museum hangings
13. Film star Humphrey
16. Litterbox user

18. Be all gloomy
21. _____ account
22. Toaster waffle brand
23. Meal fit for a pig
24. Shout
25. Makes mirrors misty
27. She's got a wool coat
28. Got a better car, perhaps
31. Camry or Corolla
32. Breakfast-all-day chain, familiarly
37. Nickname of the first Republican president

39. "Love _____ " (hit for The B-52's)
41. "Yeah, right!"
42. Tra _____ (singing refrain)
43. Easy-Bake, for one
44. Supposedly insane Roman ruler
45. Part of QED
46. Faucet
47. "It was 20 years _____ today..."

ACROSS

1. Trodden trail
5. Personal
8. Delivered an unreturnable serve
12. Spread on a roll
13. Membership charge
14. Christmas trio
15. "The Muppet Show" host
18. Slip
19. "Prison Break" extra
20. Swine's confines
21. Scrape together
24. Start of the song "Mother"
25. Work on a bootee
26. Light rain
27. He had a nephew named Poindexter
31. Carl Sandburg work
32. Needs nursing
33. Huffington Post buyer
34. Brings on board
36. Some clones
39. "The Birdman of Alcatraz"
41. Without warmth
43. Public service animal
46. Big shindig
47. Sign of summer
48. Beige
49. Having no siblings
50. Bar subject
51. Gather with a scythe

DOWN

1. Elbows
2. Danger notice
3. "_____ and the Pirates"
4. _____ sapiens
5. Many times, poetically
6. Soaked
7. Radar O'Reilly's favorite drinks
8. Radio switch
9. Jay and the Americans hit
10. One with a swelled head
11. Summarize
16. Farsi speaker, maybe
17. Typesetting units
22. Combine

23. Perfume base
25. Royal Dutch Airlines
26. TV hosts
27. Butler's assistant
28. Sushi selection
29. Rush off
30. Borden beast
31. Make a profitable move in Monopoly
34. Subtle tone

35. Virgil creation
36. Gangster's gun
37. Befuddled aunt on "Bewitched"
38. Waffle topping
40. Authorize
42. "Good buddy"
44. Drink in the bag
45. "_____ now, brown cow"

45 | Home Games

ACROSS

1. Copier paper purchase
5. Bikini part
8. _____ Gehrig
11. Minimal effort
12. Has a bug
14. Carry-_____ (luggage)
15. MLB Triple Crown winner in 1966
18. Like yarns or webs
19. Source of poi
20. Feeling of rage
22. Toil away
26. "Eureka!"
29. Way out there
30. Like the Sahara
31. With 33-Across, MLB Triple Crown winner in 1956
33. See 31-Across
35. Ms. Brockovich
36. _____ Paese cheese
37. _____ Francisco
38. Roomy auto
40. Bug in a hobby farm
41. Maker of the first all-rubber basketball
43. Home to most of Turkey

47. MLB Triple Crown winner in 1922 and 1925
52. Santa _____ winds
53. Inheritors of the Earth, in the Bible
54. _____ podrida (spicy stew)
55. Danson of "Cheers"
56. Magazine staffers: abbr.
57. "This _____ in Baseball" (Fox show)

DOWN

1. Ring official, for short
2. Used to listen
3. "Quickly!" on a memo
4. Waiter's handout
5. Milky Way or Mars
6. One causing civil unrest
7. Jessica of "Sin City"
8. _____ Angeles
9. Beatle bride Yoko
10. Admiral's org.
13. Knighted ones
16. Bowie's weapon
17. Ryan who tossed 7 no-hitters
21. Tampa Bay player

23. Liberal _____
24. "This Old House" host Bob
25. Churchill's successor
26. Iowa State's city
27. Add to the staff
28. Etcher's fluid
32. Unprincipled sort
33. "Eight _____ Out" (1988 baseball movie)
34. Place to exchange vows
36. Soaked in the tub

39. 1961 AL batting champ _____ Cash
42. Fortune-teller's words
44. Winter blanket
45. Castaway's home
46. "_____ was I ere I saw Elba"
47. Lab maze runner
48. U2 hit in 1992
49. _____ about (wander)
50. Gives approval to
51. Shaggy Tibetan beast

46 | Homophone Time

ACROSS

1. Diversion
8. Some jabs
13. Aimed upward
14. Open courtyards
15. Complaining salesman?
17. Actress Redgrave
18. "Sail _____ Ship of State": Longfellow
19. Opening wager
20. Power brokers
22. Remove abruptly
24. See eye to eye
27. It fits in a lock
28. Grazing spot
31. Litter from next of kin?
34. Clerical garment
35. Pub potable
36. Violin-playing comedian Jack
37. Breakfast pastry
39. Ancient Chinese dynasty
40. Cause of a bad air day
42. Debt letters
44. Word on many a coupon
48. Coach who's lost her voice?
51. Inception
52. Home of the Blue Jays
53. Singer Cline
54. Yoga goal

DOWN

1. Component ratchet
2. Drained of color
3. "Wheel of Fortune" option
4. Less resonant
5. Anger
6. Some office e-mail
7. "I Dream of Jeannie" star
8. Resinous secretion
9. "Fargo" producer Coen
10. Part of FDR
11. Salon job
12. Appease fully
16. Kind of flush
21. Mount Everest lies on its border
23. Caribbean resort near Venezuela
24. Triumphant cry
25. Salon supply

26. Beef cut
27. Shout of approval
29. One billion years
30. Whichever
32. "Kukla, Fran and
_____"
33. Stress
38. Fairy tale meanies
39. Mackinac Island's lake

40. "Little _____ of Horrors"
41. "_____ Lisa Smile"
43. "Beetle Bailey" dog
45. Comic Meara
46. Nov. 11 honorees
47. Greek god of love
49. Hog home
50. "Butterflies _____
Free"

47 | Gooey on the Inside

ACROSS

1. Victim of melodrama
7. Playground equipment
13. Baltimore athlete
14. "S1m0ne" star Al
15. It's gooey on the inside
17. Norse capital
18. About, in memos
19. Part of, as a plot
20. "That's _____ ask!"
24. Refreshingly new
28. TV site, often
30. With 32-Across, it's gooey on the inside
32. See 30-Across
33. Plane's path
35. Italian sauce
36. Rips off
37. "Pronto!": abbr.
39. March Madness source: abbr.
40. Over and one
44. It's gooey on the inside
49. Louisiana demographic
50. Punctual
51. Official messenger
52. Shy loch resident

DOWN

1. Practice area for martial arts
2. Greek war deity
3. Pepper grinder
4. Work alone
5. '60s TV Tarzan
6. Escorted from the front door
7. Rejected
8. Hourly pay
9. I, in Innsbruck
10. Diarist Anaïs
11. African antelope
12. Elbow-bender
16. _____ about (roughly)
19. "Casablanca" heroine
20. Composer Thomas
21. Lane in Metropolis
22. TV series with Evangeline Lilly
23. Online view intro
24. State south of Virg.

25. River that begins with Pittsburgh
26. Sink or swim
27. Slippery swimmers
29. "Li'l Abner" creator Al
31. Made into law
34. Jacob's twin
38. Producer Spelling
39. Carter of "Gimme a Break"
40. Poker prizes
41. Hertz competitor
42. Highway truck
43. Shoe insert
44. Bach's "bah"
45. Prefix with historic
46. P of mph
47. Mauna _____, Hawaii
48. U-turn from SSW

48 | Cubic Zirconia

ACROSS

1. Limber
6. RN treatment
9. Demand, as a price
12. FedEx won't deliver to one
13. Written hugs
14. On the _____ vive (watchful)
15. Vigor
16. Cut of cubic zirconia
18. Cleo's snake
19. Big basin
21. Les _____-Unis (the United States, in France)
22. "_____ the season . . ."
23. Goof up
24. Cut of cubic zirconia
28. _____ Chen shoes
31. Leave at the altar
32. Winter mo.
33. Pineapple plantation island
34. The sun, personified
35. Cut of cubic zirconia
37. Calif. airport
39. Peas' place
40. "Watch it wiggle, see it jiggle" dessert
43. Society newcomer
44. Genesis vessel
47. Cut of cubic zirconia
49. Counterindicate
51. En preceders
52. Culpa preceder
53. Like a vacuum
54. Kind of flour or whiskey
55. Cheer of a sort
56. Deceptive ploys

DOWN

1. Grp. for Nancy Lopez
2. Acknowledgments of debt
3. Cook's meas.
4. On everyone's wish list
5. Foreign
6. Pyramid, to a pharaoh
7. Extended time off from wk.
8. Cider-making device
9. Light greenish blue
10. Executive, slangily
11. Bride's greeting
17. Fiscal time frame: abbr.
20. Having had experience in
22. "Falling Skies" network

23. Getaway
24. Slumber party wear, for short
25. Spanish river
26. Not well
27. Consult
28. Glass vessel
29. "I guessed it!"
30. Rustic affirmative
33. Quaint
36. Robin Hood, for one
37. Camera type: abbr.
38. Lather-laden
40. Fan's disapproval
41. TV award
42. _____ majesty (act of treason)
43. WWII milestone
44. Swiss peaks
45. Solemn act
46. Custodian's jinglers
48. Actress Thompson
50. Flightless fowl in the outback

ACROSS

1. Top dog
6. NASDAQ, for one
9. Parts of gals.
12. Ancient Greek physician
13. Air: pref.
14. OPEC member
15. On _____-to-know basis
16. Apple pie order?
18. Home, food, and fashion magazine
20. Elephant's weight, maybe
21. Apprehensive feeling
25. Mex. miss
28. Bluish green
31. Stephen of "V for Vendetta"
32. "Sophisticated" fashion magazine
35. "... _____ quit!"
36. Court plea, informally
37. Nothing doing?
38. Beguile
40. Strike caller, for short
42. Publication that shares its title with a Thackeray novel
48. It might come on a blue plate
51. Large U.S. bakery
52. Dog mitt
53. CD predecessors
54. Subject for an X-file
55. Amber, e.g.
56. Govt. agency that has your number
57. Bad impressions?

DOWN

1. Gelatin substitute
2. Sprinter's assignment
3. "Guilty," e.g.
4. Shoe lift
5. "_____ to bed"
6. "Yes, _____!"
7. Food for sea urchins
8. Refrain from singing?
9. Quid pro _____
10. Little bit
11. "Get it?"
17. Rest room sign
19. Foreword, for short
22. Mortarboard wearer, briefly
23. 1995 triple Grammy winner

24. Container weight
25. Ruined
26. Not common
27. Shade
29. Night school subj.
30. Roughly
33. Necessitates
34. Data compression format
39. Plastic pipe material, briefly
41. "Oops! Sorry about that!"
43. Siestas
44. She requested "As Time Goes By"
45. 2006 role for Whitaker
46. "Yeah, sure!"
47. Reagan and Howard
48. Place to relax
49. Buddy
50. Lamb's mother

50 | Time for Bed

ACROSS

1. Convention handout
8. Suggestions
13. Digestive enzyme that breaks down starch into sugar
14. Bill of fare
15. One who takes a bow?
16. Chew the scenery
17. Sixth sense, for short
18. Flight data: abbr.
20. No longer working: abbr.
21. Brand of drywall
24. "_____ we having fun yet?"
25. Ran into
26. Sampler of food
28. Swing wildly
31. Warty swamp hoppers
32. Johnny _____, former lead singer of The Sex Pistols
34. Meditative sect
35. Aardvark's morsel
36. Brand of makeup
41. FX field in the movies
42. Mozart's "Il mio tesoro," e.g.
43. Lobster coral
44. Hawaiian starch staples
46. Mobile home?
49. 15-percenter
50. Found
51. Takes a drubbing
52. Sound investments?

DOWN

1. Church areas
2. Plain folk
3. Mr. Magoo, e.g.
4. Annex
5. _____ chi (martial art)
6. Declare with confidence
7. Reach
8. Peggy Fleming or Kristi Yamaguchi
9. '60s war zone, briefly
10. Proportionately
11. Pronounced
12. Wobbles
19. Do film work, perhaps

22. Give off, as light
23. Puts on the air
27. Dance partner?
28. Geometric figure with a repeating pattern
29. Back in the day
30. Decks out
33. Hide-hair connector
34. Fanatic

37. Perfume bottles
38. Boiling mad
39. Lover
40. Detective's follow-up list
45. I, to Claudius
47. "_____ Ventura: Pet Detective"
48. Setting for many a joke

51 | Too Good to Be True

ACROSS

1. Eisenhower's command: abbr.
4. Contraction before "It'll be fun!"
8. Challenge to a duel with a glove
12. Sentence part: abbr.
13. Place to hang Christmas lights
14. Iditarod finish line
15. Low-priced Monopoly avenue
17. With 20-Across, makeup advertising claim not to take too seriously
18. Cancel out
19. Seek legal action
20. See 17-Across
25. Palindromic pacifier brand
26. Publishing ID with a bar code
27. Therapeutic claim that usually doesn't live up to its name
33. Hand lotion additive
34. Night before a holiday
36. With 43-Across, food trend it's not always wise to follow
41. Jackie O's ex
42. Takes a class
43. See 36-Across
45. Dentist's request
47. "What _____ mind reader?"
48. Drift like an aroma
49. Unagi, in sushi bars
50. "I want food!" to a cat
51. Chris of "The Good Wife"
52. AMA members

DOWN

1. Dr. Guillotin, for example
2. Bad time to be woken up
3. Foldable art
4. Dollar divisions
5. "Ahoy there, _____!"
6. In vitro items
7. "_____ Blu, Dipinto Di Blu" ("Volare" alternate title)
8. "Weekend Update" show: abbr.
9. Baggy-fitting
10. Love, French-style

11. Lap dog, for short
16. Piercing locale
21. Canadian NHLer
22. Take advantage of
23. "30 Rock" network
24. Hairy antelope
28. "Too-Ra-Loo-Ra-Loo-_____" (song also called "Irish Lullabye")
29. Brewhouse brew
30. Corn center
31. _____ beans: nachos ingredient

32. Boxer Holyfield
35. Ford flops of the '50s
36. Felony
37. "Old MacDonald" refrain
38. "_____ my heart in San Francisco..."
39. Like J, in the alphabet
40. Swerve off course
41. Radio personality Carolla
44. "I _____ a Putty Tat" (1947 animated short)
45. Hold title to
46. Kung _____ chicken

52 | You Complete Me

ACROSS

1. Haiku, for one
5. Adobe file extension
8. Bind with a band
12. "O, beware, my lord, of jealousy" speaker
13. Sound receptor
14. Sound bounce
15. Online dial
16. Completely
18. Acclaim
20. Make a dart
21. Completely
27. "Game of Thrones" channel
30. Interplanetary transport: abbr.
31. Addition to a bill
32. Ben, in "Star Wars"
34. "Press _____ key to continue"
36. Letter that follows epsilon
37. Camera brand
39. Beer container
41. Treacherous serpent
42. Completely
44. Legal group: abbr.

45. Zing
50. Completely
55. Byte prefix
56. Word after quantum or before year
57. Bard's "before"
58. Woeful exclamation
59. Chooses
60. Jaguar model
61. Longs

DOWN

1. Prospector's tool
2. Island hit by a 6.7 earthquake in 2006
3. "Holy cow!"
4. Peter Lorre film sleuth
5. Nave seat
6. "Camptown Races" syllable
7. Campus newbie
8. "Shucks"
9. "_____ bin ein Berliner"
10. P, to Pythagoras
11. Wolf relative
17. Look from a wolf
19. RV center?
22. Birds-feather connector
23. Maker of toy trucks

24. Entrepreneur's start
25. "Why don't we?"
26. Duffer's challenge
27. Partner's share, perhaps
28. French word on some
    salad dressings
29. Versailles eye
33. Shop grippers: hyph.
35. Si, in Sonora
38. Swedish pop group
40. 1964 Ronny and the
    Daytonas hit

43. Type of paint
46. Approve
47. Four laps around the
    track, generally
48. Orchestrate
49. "Bonanza" character
50. "Alice" spinoff
51. Workout unit, for short
52. Muffin material
53. "Mork & Mindy" planet
54. Tappan _____ Bridge

MEDIUM

ACROSS

1. At peace
5. Jack in "Rio Lobo"
9. Exec's degree: abbr.
12. "Diamonds _____ Girl's Best Friend"
13. Anakin Skywalker's daughter
14. Poetic dusk
15. 1994 Olympics skating star
18. Maui greeting
19. "Elle" edition
20. Columbus Day month: abbr.
22. _____ canto
23. Summer cooler
26. Loathe
28. Dian Fossey subjects
32. 1976 Olympics skating star
35. Cain in "Lois & Clark"
36. Doctoral exam
37. Joe of The Flatlanders
38. "_____ Loves You"
40. Small inlet
42. Drive in Beverly Hills
45. Lively on "Gossip Girl"
49. 1984 Olympics skating star
53. Beta beater
54. "Waking Ned Devine" setting
55. Hugh Laurie's alma mater
56. Crock-_____
57. Thin
58. "The Lion King" lioness

DOWN

1. Miracle site in John 2:1
2. Inland Asian sea
3. NBC talk-show host
4. "_____ Man" Village People song
5. Caribou's kin
6. Jamie _____ Curtis
7. Televise
8. Antoinette or Osmond
9. Ryan and Tilly
10. Bridges in "Norma Rae"
11. Heche of "Hung"
16. Sail in style
17. Koran's religion
21. Sierra Nevada lake
22. Joy of "The View"
23. Use a calculator

24. Fawn's mother
25. Historic chapter
27. Norse god of war
29. "American _____" (1999 film)
30. Arm measurement
31. Crazy like a fox
33. Beginning
34. Suspect's story
39. "_____ Rwanda" (2004 film)
41. Tim in "Wild Hogs"
42. Invitation initials
43. Eight, in Madrid
44. Verb for thou
46. "A Bug's Life" princess
47. "Celebration" group _____ & the Gang
48. Sicilian city
50. Hasten
51. Notre Dame's Parseghian
52. "It's Raining _____" (1982 hit song)

54 | Stick Together

ACROSS

1. Play by ear
7. "Pretty good!
13. Free from care
14. Mrs. who owned a Chicago cow
15. Snooze under a sombrero
16. "Dennis the _____"
17. It sticks to an envelope, with 28-Across
19. 2006 Pixar movie
22. Stretch of history
23. Spilled the beans
27. Soccer chant
28. See 17-Across
30. Angry fan's shout
31. Man of steel?
33. Broadway whisper
35. It sticks to the roof of your mouth, with 37-Across
37. See 35-Across
38. Coldplay producer Brian _____
39. Flat _____ pancake
40. They stick together
45. Racetrack advisor
46. Clothing shopper's concern
47. Inflict on
49. Distinctive air
50. Toledo-to-Detroit dir.
51. Beer, informally
52. "Take _____ leave it!"
53. Hall once of "The Tonight Show"
54. Respond to a bore

DOWN

1. Existed
2. "Lord, is _____?" (Last Supper question)
3. Wedding notice word
4. Sounds of shock
5. "That's all there _____ it!"
6. Sugar bowl, creamer, etc.
7. Emphatic refusal
8. Designer Cassini
9. Religious belief
10. Ewe said it!
11. Circle section

12. Go from brunette to blonde
18. Carol syllable
19. Large co.
20. Skin moisturizer
21. C&W's McEntire
24. Memorial notice
25. Deposit for one
26. Busy one
28. Job for a daredevil
29. Take a breather

32. Low rating
34. Be available
36. Chewy candy
37. Like fishers' hooks
40. Boxing match
41. Continental coin
42. Orange throwaway
43. Nickelodeon "Explorer"
44. Meat and potatoes
45. Mai _____
48. Admit

55 | Cheap Tickets

ACROSS

1. Popular breakfast restaurant: abbr.
5. Kind of test
9. Not many
12. Conference _____
13. Log-cutting tools
14. Travel time: abbr.
15. Ballpark benches
18. Freebie seeker
19. Moved slowly to the top
20. Have a hamburger
22. One _____ time
23. Sea bordered by Yemen
27. Baseball commissioner Selig
30. Theater section
34. Popular
35. Song written by Queen Lili'uokalani
36. Paranormal ability: abbr.
39. Fictional news show on "Murphy Brown"
40. From long ago
44. Phytoplankton, e.g.
48. Kids' area on "The Howdy Doody Show"
50. Spoiled
51. It may explode when split
52. Canal between Albany and Buffalo
53. Place for a facial
54. Pear variety
55. Check one's e-mail, say

DOWN

1. Minuteman, for one: abbr.
2. Video game saga of Master Chief
3. Pancake topper
4. Sugar pill, sometimes
5. Derisive cry
6. Corporate head: abbr.
7. _____ cotta
8. It has value
9. Accomplishment
10. Rebuke to Brutus
11. Bald-faced hornet, actually
16. Part of a bicycle mechanism
17. Air-quality org.
21. Son of Abe Lincoln
23. Volcanic deposit
24. Old carmaker

25. Do something
26. Derrick Rose's org.
27. Feathery scarf
28. Popular card game
29. Pre-Easter purchase
31. Former presidential candidate Landon
32. Dedicated
33. Story about monsters
36. Richard Strauss's "Ich wollt _____ Sträusslein binden"

37. Fancy menu bird
38. _____ the test
40. Manhunt announcements: abbr.
41. Kind of tide
42. Show-off's exclamation
43. They may clash
45. "American Gigolo" star Richard
46. Operatic number
47. Looked at
49. "Mad Men" network

56 | Let's Talk

ACROSS

1. Topic of talk among women
6. "Memoirs _____ Geisha"
9. _____ Mahal
12. Moon-related
13. Entirely
14. Lemon or lime suffix
15. Jack of "The Great Dictator"
16. Topic of talk among women
18. Topic of talk among women
20. In addition
21. Alters, as text
23. Blue hue
27. Lyricist Gershwin
30. Cry of disgust
31. Corrosion sign
32. Topic of talk among women
34. Topic of talk among women
36. Topic of talk among women
37. Death notice, for short
38. Enero or Julio
40. Give it a shot
41. Computer entry
42. Beaucoup lead-in
44. _____-mo
46. Topic of talk among women
50. Topic of talk among women
54. Rajah's wife
55. Rainy
56. No longer working: abbr.
57. '70s VP Spiro
58. Fireman's tool
59. One way to order a martini
60. Topic of talk among women

DOWN

1. Many
2. Drought-tolerant plant
3. "_____ Dinka Doo" (Durante tune)
4. Lacks wisdom
5. Avaricious
6. Lummox
7. Shoes with no heels
8. In addition
9. _____ chi
10. Hubbub

11. Aniston, to friends
17. Stockpile
19. Neeson of "Kinsey"
22. Topics of talk among women, for this puzzle
24. Give up, as smoking
25. _____-friendly
26. Court fig.
27. Apple shuffler
28. "Malibu Country" star
29. Toiling away
33. Hide away
35. Squishy sports brand

39. Sacred Egyptian beetle
42. Lawn cutter
43. Adult insect
45. British house member
47. "I'm _____ mood to argue"
48. Garlic relative
49. Trees yielding elastic wood
50. Bygone airline inits.
51. Irritate
52. Fr. holy woman
53. Sow site

57 | Foreign Foods

ACROSS

1. Border county in North Carolina
5. Crystal-ball gazer's phrase
9. Overly shy
12. Ticket souvenir
13. Close
14. Presidential nickname
15. Othello's "ancient"
16. Damaged, in a way
17. Rend
18. Pain grillé
21. Thanksgiving veggie
22. Played for a sucker
25. Pepper or York: abbr.
28. Student driver?
30. Substitute
31. Kahve
34. Sigourney Weaver sci-fi flick
35. Gaslight _____
36. New Deal monogram
37. Musical TV series
38. Tenth month: abbr.
40. Arroz
47. Cow utterance
49. Family ladies
50. "American _____"
51. Antelope with a mane
52. Diamond Head locale
53. Jail unit
54. Came across
55. Carpentry class
56. "_____ Plus 8"

DOWN

1. Skeptic's retort
2. Hot body?
3. Bigger than the both of us
4. Dark, durable wood
5. Narrow strip of land
6. Chance
7. Mark's replacement
8. Sicilian volcano
9. Hauls away
10. Japanese sash
11. Cowboy's okay
19. Cruise ship accommodation
20. Catch a ride to the beach?
23. Marked, as a ballot
24. One who tints fabrics
25. Buck

26. Noisy shore bird
27. Auditions
29. "_____ Stoops to Conquer"
30. Prepare eggs, in water
32. Stronghold
33. Confuse
39. Treat's alternative
41. Old Testament book after Joel
42. Flood survivor
43. "It seems to me," in computerese: abbr.
44. Personal view
45. Farm newborn
46. Fashion magazine founded in 1945
47. Producer of many movie musicals
48. Single person

58 | Any Way You Slice It

ACROSS

1. Towers on the highway: abbr.
4. 1975 Wimbledon winner
8. Butterflies' homes
12. 14 degrees Fahrenheit, in Celsius
14. End of a Latin 101 trio
15. One disturbed by a pea
16. Area _____
17. Jeff MacNelly comic
18. Desi Arnaz's daughter
19. Stick (out)
21. Shape with two parallel sides
24. Since
26. Buttery cracker
27. iPod model
28. 15-, 21-, 36-, or 46-Across, for a diamond
29. Little bits of charge
33. Clothing
35. "Sounds like a plan"
36. Fantastic
41. Property _____
42. Bind again
43. "I screwed up"
45. Hippie's agreement
46. French noblewoman
50. One on either side of Clinton?
51. When many people watch football
52. Brightly lit sign
53. "Righto"
54. Female in the field

DOWN

1. Intensify, with "up"
2. Let out
3. Jennifer of "The Good Girl"
4. Fancy tie
5. Point (toward)
6. "_____ Just Not That into You"
7. Chekov, on "Star Trek": abbr.
8. Places to soak and relax
9. It merged with BP in 1998
10. Forearm bones
11. Majestic horse
13. Durham sch.
18. Permit
19. She was often jealous of Marcia

20. Olympics cheer
22. Island mentioned in "Kokomo"
23. Dug trap
25. Automobile safety feature
28. Dernier _____
30. Where picnics are held
31. Piece keepers?: abbr.
32. Survey question answered with one of two letters
34. Bar choice
36. Illegal payoff
37. Revisited
38. Formal announcement of arrival
39. Like some mythology
40. Chef's lid
44. It's often groaned at
46. French pronoun
47. Question response: abbr.
48. Popular horror movie franchise
49. Someone might have one for detail

59 | Give the Boot

ACROSS

1. "CSI" network
4. "Anna and the King" setting
8. Pal
12. What you might put your ducks in
13. Word in a proof
14. _____ day (Wednesday)
15. Grow older
16. Fix firmly
17. Mischievous urchins
18. Waterproof boot
21. Singer Lovett
22. Alanis Morissette hit
26. _____-Lorraine (area in northeast France)
30. Missile's path
31. Boots popular among the modern Vogue Goth
35. Sphere
36. Kind of cookies
37. Holding account
39. "The Office" actor Idris _____
43. Workout boots
47. Cigar remnant
50. Choice on "Let's Make a Deal"
51. Diving seabird
52. News you can use
53. It connects to the elbow
54. Mlle. who's been canonized
55. Cease
56. Dead skin removal
57. Cut down forests

DOWN

1. Move like an earwig
2. Four on a par three
3. Grow larger, as a population
4. Penultimate contest
5. Butterfly or Maiden preceder
6. On pins and needles
7. Mrs. Gomez Addams
8. Lightweight cotton fabric
9. Sing without knowing the words
10. Man behind the plate: abbr.
11. AWOL trackers
19. Security issue
20. Vacuum cleaner brand
23. Scottish refusal

24. Letters on some as-is mdse.
25. Adds to an e-mail
27. _____ Square (Atlanta shopping mall)
28. Took the foot off the accelerator
29. NYPD alert
31. "_____ is me!"
32. Tax agency: abbr.
33. Brian Williams's network
34. Store

38. Early modern jazz style
40. Tether
41. Big bully
42. Out of order
44. Kind of model
45. "The _____ Ranger"
46. Kind of hygiene
47. Ashlee, to Jessica
48. "The Closer" network
49. Mysterious hoverer: abbr.

60 | Burning Desire Within

ACROSS

1. Oil additive
4. Kind of tournament
8. Cathedral nook
12. To boot
13. West Alaskan seaport
14. Go smoothly
15. Surrealist Jean
16. Unconscious state
17. Intense anger
18. Top 40 offering
21. Variety show
22. Like Niagara Falls
23. Biblical garden
24. Mop's companion
26. Over a long time
32. Metal-bearing minerals
33. _____ about (roughly)
34. Help the economy
37. They sing near sopranos
38. "Winter Wonderland" clergyman
41. Mrs. David Copperfield
42. Thumbs-down reactions
43. Mont. neighbor
45. Play segments
46. "Take _____ your leader"
47. Time out for tots
48. Actress lone
49. Sparkle
50. Hurricane hub

DOWN

1. RR terminal
2. Undersea weapon
3. Puffy pastry
4. When prompted
5. Swim meet locale
6. Oscar winner Thompson
7. Close shave
8. Kinky coifs
9. Herbarium specimen
10. Soaked
11. She sheep
19. Pint-sized
20. Missile housing
21. Flag thrower, at times
24. "So sorry"

25. "You _____ what you eat"
27. Years on end
28. Manhattan neighborhood, like SoHo
29. What vines do
30. Lunchtime, typically
31. AMA members
34. Enterprise officer

35. Political group
36. Wipe away
37. Burning desire hidden in three answers
39. Christmas, in carols
40. Alpha follower
41. _____ Kapital
44. Do an impression of

61 | Gone to the Dogs

ACROSS

1. Wheat and oat _____
6. Be bedridden
9. Double-crosser
12. "The Faerie Queene" division
13. Bill and _____
14. Abbr. in car ads
15. Small dog breed named after a state in Mexico
17. Embitterment
18. Meddle
19. Foldable mattress
21. Mercury or Saturn
25. One paying a flat fee?
26. "If I _____ the world..."
27. Bull's-eye hitter
28. Eye amorously
29. Small dog breed with a short-muzzled face and a curly tail
30. _____ agreement
34. Pain in the neck
36. Play loudly
37. _____ ID
40. Plan to spend
41. Cut's partner
42. Place for a stud?
43. Gun, as an engine
44. Small dog breed nicknamed "wiener dog"
50. "We're number _____!"
51. Biblical suffix
52. Stun gun
53. "Spy vs. Spy" magazine
54. "The Matrix" hero
55. What some trees provide

DOWN

1. Abbr. atop some e-mails
2. "Go team!"
3. Singer DiFranco
4. To the _____ power
5. Made more powerful, with "up"
6. Stiff and sore
7. Promise to pay
8. Casual Friday shoe
9. Indian yogurt dip
10. It has strings attached
11. Ex-senator Lott
16. Frick collection
20. Numerous

(Crossword grid with numbered cells: 1-2-3-4-5, 6-7-8, 9-10-11 across top row; 12, 13, 14; 15, 16, 17; 18, 19-20; 21-22-23-24, 25; 26, 27; 28, 29, 30-31-32-33; 34-35, 36; 37-38-39, 40; 41, 42; 43, 44-45, 46-47-48-49; 50, 51, 52; 53, 54, 55)

21. Country club figure
22. Big galoot
23. "Th-th-that's _____, folks!"
24. Object in a haystack?
25. Kind of team
27. Grooved on
29. Good thing to break
31. Sleazy paper
32. "Roses _____ red . . ."
33. "_____ them eat cake!"
35. Blush

36. Pops, like a bubble
37. Storage medium
38. Hippodrome, e.g.
39. Dwelt
40. "Phooey!"
42. Bounce back, in a way
45. Devoured
46. "Fat chance!"
47. Cable network
48. "Waking _____ Devine" (1998 film)
49. Dr. of rap

62 | We Are Family

ACROSS

1. Autobahn autos
5. _____ Pet
9. Faculty levels, for short?
12. "Hellzapoppin'" actress Martha
13. _____ Mason (asset management firm)
14. Crackpot
15. Unclothed
17. 50 Cent piece?
18. Agnesë Gonxhe Bojaxhiu, familiarly
20. Yemen's capital
21. Sit in on, as a class
22. 1958 Rosalind Russell comedy
26. Govt. code crackers: abbr.
27. Hamilton is on it
28. Chemistry or biology: abbr.
31. A Boy Scout may tie one
35. Head of Harpo Productions
38. Annuls
39. Musical group whose biggest hit is also this puzzle's title
43. Off-road transport: abbr.
44. Accusatory words
46. Mountain pass
47. The Dakotas, once: abbr.
48. Dolls since 1961
49. Season opener?
50. Competitor of Bloomie's
51. Stair unit

DOWN

1. Support _____
2. Kenyan rebels from the 1950s
3. 1992 country album by one of the Judd family
4. Usher to, as a table
5. Professor Plum's game
6. München Mr.
7. Belinda Carlisle's "_____ Weak"
8. Shining brightly
9. How some losses are shown
10. Somewhat
11. Annual parade honoree, for short
16. Spicy cuisine choice
19. Wish undone
20. _____ Andreas Fault

23. O'Hare info: abbr.
24. Chaps
25. Gloucester's cape
28. "Hangle: A cluster of coat hangers," e.g.
29. Prescription cough medicine ingredient
30. Lesley Gore's "_____ My Party"
31. Hood's rod
32. Butler and Akins
33. Part of Y.S.L.
34. Photography store stock
35. Missouri River tributary
36. They can be full of falafel
37. Answers an invitation, briefly
40. Perlman of "Cheers"
41. Cutty _____
42. Parts of words: abbr.
45. Psychic's claim: abbr.

63 | Adorn It All!

ACROSS

1. Miss America accessory
5. "Jumbo" plane
8. Toss with a spatula
12. What an expectant father might do
13. "Days of _____ Lives"
14. Overdue
15. Adorning wristband with danglers
18. Houston ballplayer
19. School finals
20. Reef material
24. Adornment worn in a lapel
28. Labyrinth
32. All you need, in a Beatles song
33. Mean Amin
34. Prayer ending
35. Stringed toy: hyph.
36. Facial adornment
38. Put off until later
39. Pal of Kukla and Fran
43. Capri and Wight, for two
48. Adorning string of precious stones
52. Scarlett's home
53. _____ mode

54. Govt. workplace watchdog
55. NBA star O'Neal's nickname
56. X3 and X5 automaker
57. "To _____ it may concern"

DOWN

1. Adoption org. for 11-Down
2. Oohs and _____
3. "Shoo!"
4. Frau's husband
5. Monster.com listing
6. 31-Down's continent: abbr.
7. With 9-Down, refrain syllables
8. Show off one's biceps
9. See 7-Down
10. Couple in gossip columns
11. Household animals
16. Tease by imitating
17. Animation frame
21. Express one's views
22. No longer plagued by
23. Absinthe flavor

24. Stallone's nickname
25. "Is that _____ much to ask?"
26. Climbing vine
27. Corp. VIP
28. Feb. follower
29. "Who _____ to argue?"
30. Buddhist sect
31. Where Wimbledon is: abbr.
37. Actor Estrada
38. Costa _____ Sol

39. Makes a choice
40. Wife of Jacob
41. "Tomb raider" Croft
42. Baghdad's land
44. School zone sign
45. Mascara's place
46. Reverberate
47. Stitched line
49. Arrest
50. Shade tree
51. Crow cry

64 | Hollywood Crossword

ACROSS

1. Baby seals
5. Is for many
8. Precious
12. Home to Columbus
13. Long in "Big Momma's House"
14. River of Tuscany
15. Arena in Lexington, Kentucky
16. "My _____ Skip" (2000)
17. ABBA ballerina
18. Best Picture of 2009
21. _____ de France
22. Bard's "before"
23. Le Carre's "The Tailor of _____"
26. Wimbledon winner Williams
30. In the past
31. Totality
32. Ethel of "Anything Goes"
36. Warren of "Love Affair"
39. "Mamma Mia!" role
40. Corn spike
41. Heidi Klum reality show
48. Move, in realty jargon
49. Hold the deed
50. "Jaws" boat
51. Phone co. employee
52. Twice XXVI
53. Bert of "The Wizard of Oz"
54. Playwright Hart
55. Opposite of WSW
56. Changed hair color

DOWN

1. After-dinner wine
2. "No can do": hyph.
3. Prop for Sherlock
4. Loren in "Two Women"
5. Martin in "My Big Fat Greek Wedding"
6. Uprising
7. "Take It Easy" group
8. Hoofer
9. "The Phantom of the Opera" phantom
10. Hathaway in "Get Smart"
11. Greeting from Leo
19. Einstein's birthplace
20. Mining extract

23. Tillis of Nashville
24. Mature
25. Neither fish _____ fowl
27. Superlative suffix
28. Loony tune
29. Madigan in "Field of Dreams"
33. "M*A*S*H" brass
34. Foamy brew
35. Kidman in "Australia"
36. Mac in "Soul Men"

37. _____ de Cologne
38. "Torch Song Trilogy" hero
41. Dance with a queen
42. Emilio Estevez movie "_____ Man" (1984)
43. World Cup cheers
44. Artemis, to Apollo
45. Fay in "King Kong"
46. Dull pain
47. "The Longest _____" (2005 movie)

65 | Veggies Only

ACROSS

1. Divine in "Hairspray"
5. Mirror-conscious
9. Lynus in "Lost"
12. Itchy fabric
13. Taj Mahal city
14. Draft pick?
15. Vegetarian singer of "Alison"
18. Colorful marine gastropod
19. "Annie Hall" director
20. "A Bridge _____ Far"
21. Pat on the buns?
22. Snake that killed Cleopatra
25. 1970s fad dance
27. Prod
30. Vegetarian leader of The Pretenders
33. Glum drop?
34. "Penny _____" (Beatles hit)
35. Miss Piggy, for one
36. Like a doily
38. Waitress at Mel's Diner
40. "Ethan Frome" novelist Wharton
42. Appraise
46. Vegetarian singer of "Theology"
48. "The Gold-Bug" author
49. Manicurist's implement
50. Carbonated quaff
51. More than mos.
52. Silo stock
53. They may be split

DOWN

1. Females bearing 12-Across
2. 1996 also-ran
3. "Super" star
4. Top-tier celebrities
5. Inanely
6. Dumbfounded
7. Form 1040 org.
8. Birth-related
9. Party poppers
10. Women's fashion magazine
11. Chemist's #10
16. Unkempt ones
17. Shelley's "Adonais," e.g.
21. Like some sandwiches
22. Play part

23. "More of the Monkees" song
24. Nutty confections
26. "The Princess Diaries" princess
28. Needless fuss
29. Condensation
31. Angry, and then some
32. 1984 Lionel Richie hit
37. Threshing refuse
39. Measure of prevention
40. Behold
41. "Sack Look" designer
42. Burrowing animal
43. Prolific author?: abbr.
44. Related
45. Time pieces?
47. "_____ Hard"

66 | The Paper

ACROSS
1. Nasty
4. Disney deer
9. Renouncement of all possessions, perhaps
12. More than impress
13. Grant-_____
14. Monkey relative
15. "Halloween" director Zombie
16. "Maude" spin-off
18. Praise on a book jacket
20. Pretty soon
21. Film and TV honor
26. Clinton's second HUD secretary
27. "Do it now!": abbr.
28. Fuel efficiency measure: abbr.
31. Notes with a familiar mnemonic
33. Stat for Curt Schilling: abbr.
34. "Ahab the _____" (Ray Stevens song)
36. "I understand"
38. Destination of winning athletes?

41. Take to the sky
42. The Sorbonne, for one: Fr.
45. Oscar winner
49. Discharge static electricity
50. French article
51. Bolivia neighbor
52. Barely earn, with "out"
53. Internet portal with a butterfly logo
54. Used an Underwood
55. Victoria Beckham, _____ Adams

DOWN
1. Sharp comment
2. Military no-show
3. Work the kinks out of
4. IBM nickname
5. "Feliz _____ Nuevo!"
6. Silkscreened Andy Warhol portrait subject
7. Auction action
8. Name place
9. "Beat it!"
10. Place for free shots
11. "A Nightmare on Elm Street" creator Craven

17. "To Live and Die _____" (1985 movie)
19. Fabulous bird of myth
22. Pet, to a tot
23. Curve, as animal horns
24. Signal, in a way
25. Federal pollution police: abbr.
28. Humor magazine
29. Penitentiaries
30. Flame-based cooker
32. Color of embers
35. _____ B'rith
37. Lots of hugs, in brief
39. Straight up and down
40. Thirteen for a baker
43. Camp locale
44. Fencing weapon
45. Fall bloom
46. Timid
47. Useful hint
48. Drink with fish and chips

67 | Prints Charming

ACROSS

1. Mary _____ cosmetics
4. Sound like a dove
7. Shades of blue
12. Portuguese, e.g.
14. Like a sourpuss
15. Thaw in the Cold War
16. Forced to go
17. Dieter's yells?
19. Satisfied sighs
20. Get situated
24. Italian wine city
27. Actress Gardner
28. Put into words
29. Ancient perfumes
33. Links target
34. Squeak silencer
35. Regulation
36. Packing a punch
38. Turmoil
40. Coins a phrase or two?
45. Head honcho
48. Was taken down a peg
49. Home base for humans
50. Elvis the pelvis
51. 1990 Swayze/Moore film
52. Weep aloud
53. Fleecy female

DOWN

1. Pokes fun at
2. Labor leader I. W. _____
3. Himalayan humanoid
4. Sure thing
5. Solemn sayings
6. Draft eligible
7. Place for butts
8. Kind of
9. Net destination
10. Hearty brew
11. Barrett of Pink Floyd
13. Stay put
18. Temporary super star
21. Son of Isaac
22. Salt on a chemist's table
23. Young 'un
24. Snakes in hieroglyphics
25. "Get outta here!"

26. Okla. once
27. Leather worker's tool
30. "West Side Story" tune
31. Speak with one's hands
32. Worries
37. Leaves out
38. "Jetsons" dog
39. Uncool sort

41. Soldier's lullaby
42. Get under one's skin
43. Barrymore of "50 First Dates"
44. Eyelid ailment
45. "Family Guy" daughter
46. Root word
47. Sib

68 | Home Field Advantage

ACROSS

1. Price tag
6. Dennis the Menace, e.g.
9. Pic taker
12. Where Bowie fell
13. Whisper sweet nothings
14. "To a . . ." poem
15. Home of the Mets
17. Mantric words
18. Dazed state
19. Speaker in Cooperstown
20. Common happy hour day: abbr.
22. Dam-building org.
23. 1959 Johnny Mathis hit
24. "Hit 'em where they _____": Willie Keeler
26. Big name in printers
28. With 30-Across, home of the Blue Jays
30. See 28-Across
34. Words of denial
36. Time period for many baseball records
37. Ex post _____
40. "Wheel of Fortune" buy
42. Merino mama
43. Calls from the bleachers
44. Cockney, e.g.

46. "A boy _____ girl?"
47. Home of the Padres
50. Precursor of Microsoft Windows
51. 2008 World Series player
52. Myopic Mr. voiced by Jim Backus
53. A wee hour
54. Make a faux pas
55. Vehicles with runners

DOWN

1. Fond du _____, Wisc.
2. "Thrilla in Manila" victor
3. Cobb led the league in it 12 times
4. Mideast ruler
5. Lite
6. Polar topper
7. Suburban lawn ruiner
8. Cacao plant feature
9. _____ Field (home of the Rockies)
10. Word on a ticket
11. Like Oscar Madison
16. Follow a broker's advice, perhaps
19. Cheap-sounding
20. At a distance

21. Brazilian hot spot
23. A Pep Boy
25. Outdoor party setups
27. Like an overlook view
29. Aussie bounder
31. Like most high school grads
32. Like an inexperienced rookie
33. Bard's before
35. Joan of Arc, for one
37. Tolkien's ring-bearer
38. Homer king before Bonds

39. _____ Field (home of the Diamondbacks)
41. Elemental units
44. "Bad News" ballplayer of film
45. Birthstone for many Libras
47. Lead-in for law or med
48. Carew, seven-time AL leader in 3-Down
49. Many bout endings for 2-Down: abbr.

69 | Cooking Wisdom

ACROSS

1. Roman goddess of the moon
5. Underwear item
8. Refer to as an example
12. Notable time spans
13. _____ Cruces, New Mexico
14. Mayoral assistant
15. Get ready for printing
16. Annotation mark
18. Host of 32-Across
20. Bobby's monogram
21. Mandates
25. Corn amount
28. Thrift shop stipulation
31. India's locale
32. Popular cooking show
35. Dudley Do-Right's love
36. Real estate measure
37. Prior to, to poets
38. Affaire de coeur
40. Singer Winehouse
42. Farewell heard at the end of 32-Across
48. Seafood appetizer
51. Vicki Lawrence sitcom role
52. Diving position
53. Pen tip
54. Student's concern
55. Thoroughfare
56. Whichever
57. Pleasing

DOWN

1. "Death of a Salesman" actor Cobb
2. South Asians speak it
3. Get exactly right
4. Out and about
5. It's to the east of Bulgaria
6. Ill-considered
7. Sparkling wine center
8. Of the heart
9. Three on a sundial
10. NFL 6-pointers
11. "A mouse!"
17. Toymaker up north
19. A ways off
22. Tennis star Arthur
23. Stadium section
24. Storage place for valuables
25. Sicilian spouter

26. "Excuse me"
27. Move, briefly
29. "Monsters, _____"
30. Barely make it
33. Messed up
34. Rope fiber
39. '90s Fox sitcom
41. Arabian Peninsula country
43. Favored caretaker
44. Analogous

45. Metered ride
46. Apple computer introduced in 1998
47. Not very spicy
48. Short Red Cross course?
49. Brazilian vacation site, briefly
50. Letters on a Most Wanted poster

DIFFICULT

ACROSS

1. Beavers' work
5. "First, do no _____"
9. Send, as payment
10. Rap sheet word
12. Winter _____ (home of the czars)
13. Winter _____ (luge, et al.)
15. Jed Clampett's discovery
16. Proofreaders' marks
18. Ill humor
19. Super-secure airline
21. Nondairy milk source
22. Irish or Manx speaker
23. School attended by 007
25. Prison-related
26. Winter _____ (site of Legoland Florida amusement park)
28. Intermission
29. Dynamite inventor Alfred
30. Vientiane's land
31. "... or _____!" (threat ender)
32. Long-snouted swimmer
33. Site of Vulcan's forge
37. Eng. major's course
38. California mandarin
40. Hi-_____ graphics
41. Winter _____ (place to play instructional ball)
43. Winter _____ (starchy vegetable)
45. Laugh-a-minute folks
46. Goes bad
47. Thomas, creator of the Republican elephant
48. Has a bug

DOWN

1. Mason aide Street
2. Org. with a famous journal
3. Boom box plug-ins
4. Cowboy topper
5. In a rush
6. Barrier crossed by Hannibal
7. Carnival city
8. _____ Islands (Guam's group)
9. One way to travel
11. Ripken's record, e.g.

Across / Down clues:

12. "The Tell-Tale Heart" writer
14. Bear's advice
17. Seemingly forever
20. Flood zone sight
22. Fliers in skeins
24. iPhone no.
25. Tennis club figure
26. More moth-eaten
27. Choose not to vote
28. Starbucks worker
29. Jodie Foster title role

30. Long. crosser
32. B&B visitor
34. _____ fats
35. Top "Untouchable"
36. Hair color
38. Removes from the roster
39. Prefix with distant or lateral
42. _____ few rounds (spar)
44. It may be bookmarked

71 | Is He for Real?

ACROSS
1. Stickers
6. Photo, for short
9. Ripped to shreds
10. Burden of proof
12. Female's ideal partner
15. He was raised with Cain
16. Showtime serial drama
17. Ideal partner
21. "Alice's Restaurant" singer Guthrie
22. '50s school dance
23. Hockey legend Bobby
24. Kilt wearer
25. Female's ideal partner
27. "Don't be such _____ blanket!"
29. Roxy Music's Brian
30. Start of many California place names
33. _____-Day (vitamin brand)
34. Female's ideal partner
36. Pennsylvania, for one
38. Get one's ducks in _____

39. Female's ideal partner
43. Untruths
44. Brought home, as a salary
45. Span of history
46. Girder material

DOWN
1. Cram for an exam
2. On _____ (hot)
3. NBA official
4. No-goodnik
5. Mata Hari, for one
6. Skin opening
7. Not precise
8. Number in a Spanish quartet
9. Just not done
11. Process ore
12. Alda sitcom
13. '50s presidential inits.
14. "Seats sold out" sign
18. "Beetle Bailey" creator Walker
19. Flight board abbr.
20. Taste tester

24. Loafer or pump
25. Wander aimlessly
26. African beast that rhymes with "you"
27. Blacksmith's block
28. Frankfurter, slangily
30. Reddish-brown
31. Steer clear of

32. Politico Gingrich
33. Iowa's state tree
34. Shirt with a slogan
35. Singer Frankie or Cleo
37. Bear in the heavens
40. _____ Moines
41. Was in session
42. Opposite of post-

ACROSS

1. Bad hair day hider
4. Pulverize potatoes
8. Hairdo
12. Air conditioning measure: abbr.
13. Singer/songwriter Bates
14. Mata _____
15. "Avatar" star Worthington
16. High-stakes card game, perhaps
18. Bait holder
20. Fallujah resident
21. Windshield shades
23. Sex advice-giver Westheimer, familiarly
27. Rubber-stamp
29. Measly amount
30. Abandon a habitual defense mechanism
36. Mythical bird that carried off elephants
37. Treat for winter birds
38. Frequent flyer's woe
42. Jacket with an insignia
46. Caribbean cruise stops
48. Take on
49. Contract outs
53. On the _____ (running from the cops)
54. Automaker with a four-ring logo
55. Three-ingredient sandwiches: abbr.
56. TV cop show set in Las Vegas
57. Reared
58. Opposite of west
59. Bewitch

DOWN

1. Network that airs 56-Across
2. Big name in arcade games
3. Cougars
4. Women with young 'uns
5. Crafty person?
6. Bad-mouth
7. Surfer wannabe
8. Singing group in church
9. Acorn's destiny
10. More than exasperation
11. Tree with lights, often
17. "NO" followers
19. Information, slangily
22. Onetime rival of MGM

24. "_____ Today"
25. High craggy peak
26. 1963 title role for Paul Newman
28. "For sure!"
30. Julius Erving's nickname
31. Sturgeon eggs
32. Autumn mo.
33. Groups within groups
34. Bourjois' Illuminating _____
35. Salt Lake City's state

39. Fat, for one
40. Cigarette remains
41. Boston newspaper
43. Nothing, slangily
44. Wipe clean, in a way
45. Modify, as a soundtrack
47. Grammy-winning Fitzgerald
49. Chocolate _____
50. "Days of _____ Lives"
51. Love sonnet
52. Grounded jet

73 | Mothers of Invention

ACROSS

1. Lady Ada _____, writer of 1843 scientific paper predicting the advent of computer software
9. Play Pictionary
13. Overhead transparencies
14. Arp's art
15. German pastries
16. Psych. appraisal
17. French composer Erik
18. Leaves in the afternoon?
20. Squid fluid
21. Change for a five
22. Currency from an 18th-century nursery rhyme
24. Driver's license datum
25. POTUS to GIs
26. Feminist Germaine
27. Wrigley Field player
28. Cookie holder
29. Work
32. Sticker
33. Bible book after Gal.
36. Hunks
38. About, on a memo
39. Unruly head of hair
40. Place for a stud?
41. Pays to play
42. Geometric calculation
44. Oiliest
46. Film unit
47. Until this time
48. Weather info
49. Mary _____, patented first car windshield wiper in 1905

DOWN

1. Ropes in
2. Gasoline rating
3. Summit
4. Ornamental needle cases
5. Put on board, as cargo
6. Lunched, say
7. Boston hoopster
8. Love of Elizabeth I
9. JFK's predecessor
10. Small canyon
11. "Ten Cents _____," Rodgers and Hart song
12. Best known as Madame C. J. _____, she revolutionized the haircare and cosmetics industry for African American women
19. Dr. Virginia _____, inventor of the Newborn Scoring System

22. Bro or sis
23. "To _____ is human..."
25. Marie _____, discoverer of radium
27. Bamboozler
28. Au _____
29. Silver screen star Hedy _____, developed a transmission system during World War II
30. Silent film actress Renee _____
31. She lost her sheep

32. Eric _____, author of the "Winston Breen" series
33. Comes in
34. Magician's word
35. Charlton of "The Ten Commandments"
37. 2008 Beyoncé album, "I Am . . . _____ Fierce"
38. Worker on a comic book
41. Long (for)
43. Flight stat.
45. "_____ be an honor!"

74 | Appliance Attachments

ACROSS

1. Hearty swallow
5. Regret bitterly
8. Little green edibles
12. Pisa's river
13. Mounds of insects
15. Buff guy who makes breakfast?
17. Unrestrained shopping
18. Flow out
19. Bach instrument
22. Watering hole
26. Seminary subject
28. Lying over something
30. Horne of music
31. Stolen pane?
34. _____ about
35. He watched Rome burn
36. "Piggy" on a tot's foot
37. Willem of "Spider-Man"
39. Often poisonous plant
41. High sch. equivalency
43. Save on wedding bills
46. Wandering cook?
51. No one
52. Pilot's post
53. Prune, before drying
54. NBC sketch show
55. Type of code

DOWN

1. Toothy tools
2. Scarf or shawl
3. Facing
4. Errand runner
5. Comic actress Charlotte
6. Prefix with corn
7. French I verb
8. Arcade game
9. Spreading tree
10. Menu phrase
11. IRS info
14. Vagabond
16. By-the-book
20. Words before impasse
21. Do, re, and mi
23. Upholstery protector
24. _____ many words

25. Request from an ed.
26. Did blacksmith work
27. New Rochelle college
29. Lima's nation
32. Playbill
33. First name in Mayberry
38. Pitcher stats
40. Honolulu hello

42. Eve's grandson
44. Brazilian booter
45. Humorist Bombeck
46. Total U.S. output, e.g.
47. Internet provider letters
48. Early Beatle Sutcliffe
49. Rev
50. Conduit bend

75 | Cave Dwellers

ACROSS

1. Put 2 and 2 together, e.g.
4. AAA suggestions
8. Put your head down
12. Call in a dairy
13. Swimming wrigglers
14. Fashion monthly
15. Cave dweller at Jellystone Park
17. Short cut?
18. "Thelma & Louise" director Ridley
19. Giraffe relative with striped legs
20. Mythological cave dweller
23. Geisha's belt
24. Judges
28. "Seven Samurai" actor Toshiro
32. Nobody
33. Orbs
35. 32nd U.S. President
36. Skull Cave dweller
40. Southeast Asian capital
43. Smidges
44. Harbinger
45. V. T. Hamlin's cave dweller
48. Lead singer of U2
49. Legal declaration
50. Polynesian tuna
51. Distort, as figures
52. "Hey, you!"
53. "The Murders in the Rue Morgue" writer

DOWN

1. Pulitzer-winning poet Lowell
2. _____-wop
3. Miserable existence
4. '40s jazz genre
5. Canines, e.g.
6. Makes rhapsodic
7. Ukraine, once: abbr.
8. Tracy/Hepburn film of 1957
9. Fibula's counterpart
10. Paper _____ (fastener)
11. Visored military cap
16. Like roads in winter, often

19. Anise-flavored Greek liqueur
20. Stately splendor
21. Theatrical award
22. Short time?: abbr.
25. Hand cleaner
26. Loosen
27. Curl producer
29. So far
30. Classic soda pop
31. Early preposition

34. Oily disasters
37. A golf course may have 18
38. Irritated
39. No vote
40. Quoits targets
41. One way to run
42. Hawaiian goose
45. iPhone program, briefly
46. Discoverer's cry
47. Dessert order

ACROSS

1. Rolled-up bunches of money
5. Irish dance
8. Run _____ (in a frenzy)
12. "_____ a Kick out of You"
13. Exist
14. Unconscious state
15. Suffragette honored on U.S. stamps in 1936 and 1955
18. Port-au-Prince is its capital
19. Spooky
20. Mal _____ (seasickness)
24. Aviatrix honored with an 8-cent U.S. stamp in 1963
32. Steak order
33. Used a chair
34. Toledo's lake
35. Actress honored with a 32-cent U.S. stamp in 1995
38. Western
39. Jed Clampett player Buddy
43. Not quite right
48. Jazz singer honored with a 39-cent U.S. stamp in 2007
52. First man
53. "I do," for one
54. Cut
55. Their boughs make bows
56. Cobbler's tool
57. "So what _____ is new"

DOWN

1. Genie's offering
2. Water, to Juan
3. He loved Lucy, first name in '50s TV
4. Ballpark figure
5. Poke
6. Nest eggs inits.
7. _____-Xer
8. Tooth pain
9. Secure
10. Onetime science magazine
11. Mitty player Danny
16. Spiders' nests
17. Guam, e.g.
21. High mark with low effort

22. Intended
23. Wonderland cake message
24. Escort's offering
25. Lamb's bleat
26. "To _____ is human . . ."
27. Floral necklace
28. Chick's mother
29. Opposite of dep. at an airport
30. _____ Grande
31. Golf ball holder
36. An ex of Burt

37. Like the Sabin vaccine
39. Online bidding site
40. _____ one's time
41. Deli side dish
42. Stately trees
44. Silent performer
45. "American _____" (hit show)
46. Cuts lumber
47. "Auld Lang _____"
49. Actress Longoria
50. In that way
51. Wise bird

77 | Charming

ACROSS

1. *
4. Ball girl
7. Heiress Hilton
12. Summer in Vichy
13. "Call _____ day"
14. First class
15. Ten-sided figure
17. Group of nine
18. Slight notion
19. Church doctrine
20. Tennis call
21. Loose-_____ binder
23. Apple product
25. Actor Connery
26. English channel?
29. *
31. Boom box
33. Director Spike
34. Mentally sound
36. Indian flatbread
37. Ione of "Say Anything"
38. Price-fixing watchdog: abbr.
39. It's often eaten with wasabi
42. On the other hand
46. Virginia Woolf's "_____ of One's Own"
47. Collectively, the eight starred entries throughout this puzzle
48. *
49. Mine rock
50. A, in Berlin
51. Iditarod vehicles
52. Word before none or exam
53. Nurturing and affection, for short

DOWN

1. Prefix with cab or cure
2. Fwy. from L.A. to Phoenix
3. *
4. Pinkie
5. Alma mater to many a British royal
6. *
7. *
8. Physically or emotionally removed
9. *
10. One on an agenda
11. _____ good example
16. Smart _____ (self-assertive one)

22. "At _____!"
23. Neighbor of Ind.
24. Homer's bartender
25. "Don't move, Fido!"
26. *
27. Actress Arthur of "The Golden Girls"
28. Not pro
30. Some Alaskan natives
32. _____-nous (in confidence)

35. An unemployed person might seek one
37. Wearing footwear
38. A smaller number (than)
39. Bodily pouches
40. Asian mountain range
41. Not all
43. Juno's counterpart
44. Coat of a seed
45. 'N _____

78 | Ladies First

ACROSS

1. Key of Beethoven's Symphony No. 7: abbr.
5. Candy that comes in a dispenser
8. Distinctive doctrines
12. Common opening time
13. _____ Lilly and Co.
14. Straight, at the bar
15. How taco salad is often served
17. iPod model
18. Vanna White?
20. Peace, in Russia
21. At full speed
22. 2001 film starring 50-Across
24. Latino "light": Span.
25. Massey of classic movies
27. Emily Post?
32. Most mall rats
33. Surgery sites: abbr.
35. Friendly ghost of fame
38. "It's _____!" ("Simple!")
40. Sot's sound
41. Serena Williams?
44. Crazily
46. Propose for, as an award
47. _____ mortals
48. Wildcats of the Big 12 Conference: abbr.
49. House of _____
50. Star of 22-Across
51. Wilt
52. Pertaining to, on a memo

DOWN

1. Twenty Questions category
2. Least possible
3. Prehistoric Pueblo culture
4. Country singer Colter
5. Coop sound
6. Model Macpherson
7. Gobs and gobs
8. It's accommodating
9. Dress lines
10. Furbies in 1998, e.g.
11. Rage
16. QVC alternative
19. Get, as a job

23. Egyptian _____ (cat breed)
25. Places for some pairs
26. Golfer Hinkle or actor Chaney
28. Indy 500 letters
29. "...not always what they _____"
30. Hold in check
31. Vehicle with a lot of pull
34. Geometric solid

35. Victor
36. Evangelist McPherson
37. Show disdain for
38. Athos, to Aramis: Fr.
39. Christian music's Patty
42. The National League's Most Valuable Player in 1998
43. Self-satisfied
45. 74-time "Jeopardy!" winner Jennings

79 | Fancy Party Attire

ACROSS

1. "_____ Lazy River"
4. Stick (out)
7. With "Little" in front and 50-Across after, fancy party attire for a woman
12. Prefix with practice
13. Whichever
14. Mighty peculiar
15. Heat unit, briefly
16. Former Soviet space station
17. What 16-Across landed in after being brought down
18. Canyon edge
19. Woman's hosiery for a fancy party
21. Actress Hathaway of "The Devil Wears Prada"
23. River inlet
24. Stargazer's club: abbr.
25. Peas, in Paris
27. Woman's shoulder wrap for a fancy party
32. Do harvesting
33. Roll call vote in favor
34. XXX times X
35. River to the North Sea
37. Woman's footwear for a fancy party
43. Chaucer's far
44. "Pitfall" platform
45. "Wayne's World" denial
46. Boxer Laila, daughter of Muhammad
47. Attach again, as a brooch
48. Like some wine
49. _____ room (play area)
50. See 7-Across
51. Gender
52. Epoch of history

DOWN

1. Eclipse shadow
2. Green films
3. Women's school graduates
4. Impromptu jazz sessions
5. Apartment or condo, e.g.
6. First-timer
7. Inclined to reading and study
8. St. _____ (Caribbean island nation)

9. The sun, in ancient Egypt
10. Rugged rock formation
11. Ranges of knowledge
20. Like new dollar bills
22. Atty.'s title
25. Pie serving
26. Man-mission link
28. Street scamps
29. Sailor's assent
30. A person's fortunes
31. Office gizmo for making tags
34. Tennis great Evert
36. Susan Lucci role
37. Challenging
38. Fusion energy org.
39. Be slack-jawed
40. Finishes
41. Oral history
42. The Underworld's boundary

80 | Double Goalposts

ACROSS

1. Law enforcement alert: abbr.
4. Bogus
8. Cup covers
12. Jeer
13. Slick
14. Provide backup, perhaps
15. Music case
17. Wheat flatbread
18. Astringent medicine
20. He brought about Holy Innocents' Day
23. _____ Mountain Daredevils
24. Tamed
25. Level
28. State of ecstasy
34. Buffoons
35. Cipher
36. Ecstasy
40. Playful animal
41. Rambler
45. Cost of a hand
46. Tuna variety
50. Computer image
51. Fish for
52. Worthless trifle
53. Salamander's cousin
54. Dance in a circle
55. Brume

DOWN

1. Where "Lost" was found
2. Detachable container
3. Scrape's partner
4. Not hollow
5. Hand guard
6. Actor Guinness in "Star Wars"
7. Legend
8. Highest capital
9. One of the Balearic Islands
10. Get in the way of
11. Tail illegally
16. Stopped sleeping
19. Maximize effectiveness, as a skill
20. British ship letters
21. Big foot?
22. Gun
25. Viscosity symbol

26. Range for some TV broadcasts
27. Sounds of doubt
29. Snack
30. Montezuma, for one
31. Horse doc
32. Prior to, in poetry
33. "... _____ gloom of night..."
36. Site of the pineal gland
37. Tilting tool
38. Following behind
39. What a nose picks up
40. City destroyed in "Godzilla Raids Again"
42. Meat-and-potatoes dish
43. Margarine
44. Over, in Germany
47. Rub out
48. Earth Summit site of 1992
49. Heckler's missile

EXPERT

ACROSS

1. Gun holders
9. Pet food brand
13. Teaches a lesson to
14. Remarriage prefix
15. Tune from "Annie"
16. Do a critic's job
17. Skin opening
18. Saya Son's army
19. Short-fused
21. Lerner and Loewe title
23. ER ward
24. Like country life
25. Tune from "A Funny Thing Happened on the Way to the Forum"
31. Took to the police station
32. Lobe locale
33. Title tune in a Joel Grey musical
36. To the point
38. Get out of bed
39. Shade trees
40. Ballerina's skirt
41. Rodgers and Hammerstein title tune
45. Truck driver on the radio
46. Like some skillets
47. Long-eared hopper
48. Most pricey

DOWN

1. Excited, with "up"
2. "Deep Space Nine" character
3. Undivided amount
4. Hightail it
5. Hang back
6. "To be" to Henri
7. Classic auto
8. U-turn from NNE
9. Haifa inhabitant
10. In the least
11. Copycat's phrase
12. Completely drained
18. Govt. agent
19. _____-tac-toe
20. Prefix for system
21. Do the job

22. Elvis's middle name
24. Former Cub Sandberg
26. "Chains of Love" artist
27. "Bet you can't," e.g.
28. Become angry
29. "Yeah, right!"
30. Give it a go
33. Do an outfielder's job
34. Caribbean resort island
35. Bad dog
36. Piece of chinaware
37. "Like, no problem, man"
39. Word after who or what
41. Mil. training program
42. Herriman's Krazy feline
43. Hip hop artist and actor Def
44. Aardvark entrée

ACROSS

1. Helgenberger of "CSI"
5. Sing like Al Jarreau
9. Audiophile's collection
12. Walkie-talkie word
13. Milne bear
14. Possess, to a Scotsman
15. Spanish marchlike ballroom dance
17. Conservative Coulter
18. Courts
19. Clingy lizard
21. "Grease 2," e.g.
24. Words that follow a perfume name
25. Small bra measurement
26. American Red Cross organizer Barton
27. Me, to Miss Piggy
28. Have a date
30. Comedian Margaret
33. Circus figure
35. Hammer-wielding god
36. Tackle
38. Mail-in offer
40. Cheated out of
41. New Delhi garb
42. Paintings and such
43. Swing dance that started in the 1930s
48. Suffix meaning "follower"
49. _____ Dei ("The Da Vinci Code" group)
50. Wrapped up
51. Maple syrup, really
52. Pro _____
53. Stain

DOWN

1. Janitor's tool
2. Sinatra ex Gardner
3. Hi-_____ graphics
4. Mature
5. Thread holder
6. Corn leftovers
7. "You've got mail" ISP
8. Capricorn, in astrology
9. Latin American ballroom dance from Cuba
10. "Thanks," in Germany
11. Managuan Mr.
16. She doesn't have antlers
20. Make a misstep
21. Brady Bunch butcher
22. Prefix before "friendly" or "tourism"

23. Fast ballroom dance that combines the foxtrot and other dances
24. Shots for it contain an inactive vaccine
26. Swindle
28. Praise after finishing a task
29. Have
31. Like some salsa
32. Hematite, e.g.
34. Stan who co-created The Incredible Hulk
35. '50s 2-seaters
36. Bangkok residents
37. Heart attachment
38. Rizzo of "Midnight Cowboy"
39. Before, to a poet
41. Setting for phasers
44. Stock opening
45. Dizzy Gillespie's genre
46. Game with a "Skip" card
47. Understand

83 | Gal Pals

ACROSS

1. Coffee preference
6. WWII spy org.
9. Div. of a former union
12. Muse of lyric poetry
13. Brewer's product
15. Gal whose pal is 44-Across
16. Gal whose pal is 42-Across
17. Online marketing
19. Boxer Willard
20. Mo. on a calendar
22. Tintype tints
24. CD-_____
25. Ireland's _____ Lingus
26. Den appliance
29. Gal whose pal is 31-Across
31. Gal whose pal is 29-Across
32. "The Untouchables" composer Morricone
33. Plunk or plop preceder
34. _____ King Cole
35. Laser alternative
37. Form 1040 calc.
38. Ending with Smurf or Rock

40. "Come in!"
42. Gal whose pal is 16-Across
44. Gal whose pal is 15-Across
48. Start of a Doris Day song title
49. Like some elephants
50. Graduating class members: abbr.
51. ID digits
52. Has to have

DOWN

1. Society newbie
2. Before, to a poet
3. "_____ on a Hot Tin Roof"
4. When some news shows air
5. Auto racer A. J.
6. Less sincere
7. Place for a massage
8. More than a few: abbr.
9. Feeling the pressure, with "out"
10. Chamber workers: abbr.
11. Explorer John and actress Charlotte

14. French for "already seen"
18. Drifting
20. Glenn in the Astronaut Hall of Fame
21. Selling points in real estate
23. "Ripley's Believe _____ Not!"
24. Interstate sign: abbr.
25. Wildly
27. Actor Morales
28. Eastern holiday

30. Makeup items
31. Baltic native
33. Nairobi native
36. Boos
37. Get up
38. Gentlemen: abbr.
39. There's a holy one every yr.
41. McGregor of movies
43. "_____ Misérables"
45. Tell a tall tale
46. Like some scientists
47. T or F, e.g.

84 | By the Hour

ACROSS

1. Member of Cong., e.g.
4. Service edge
8. Start for fiction
12. Will Parker's honey
14. Cinerama successor
15. Oyster bar condiment
17. French crowd?
18. Bolt from the blue?
19. Stuff of legend
22. John Cameron Swayze was its spokesman
26. Salesperson's gift, perhaps
28. Be dependent
30. Tree used for wine stoppers
31. Policy of some schools
34. Carry _____ conversation
35. Not stirring
36. Game cry
37. Perennial resembling a primrose
39. Podded plant
41. CO zone
43. Off-guard
47. Comic strip hobo
52. Fencing tool
53. Come before
54. Caterwaul
55. Emulates Romeo
56. Part of WYSIWYG

DOWN

1. Alliance basis
2. Halitosis symptom
3. In _____ parentis
4. Impatient
5. Modern evidence, sometimes: abbr.
6. 1969 Super Bowl number
7. Mistress of Charles II
8. Home of the Herald
9. Bird featured in the logo for Birds Australia
10. Second X or O
11. Caveman's tool
13. Crooked
16. Goatlike figure
20. Stepped (on)
21. "___ Darlin'" (Conway Twitty hit)
23. Poet Van Duyn
24. Singly
25. Jaguar E-Type

26. Baby Boom successor, for short
27. Sea bordering Kazakhstan
29. Vegetable resembling a large scallion
31. Where the wild things are?
32. Inebriated
33. Official language of Jordan
38. Urge forward
40. Chest noises
42. Become liquid, perhaps
44. Forever, seemingly
45. Motor attachment?
46. Patella's place
47. "Yo!"
48. V-mail address
49. Baptist's bench
50. She recorded the concept album "Starpeace"
51. Ally of the Missouri

85 | That Certain Something

ACROSS

1. Tuscaloosa team, briefly
5. U-turn from NNE
8. Sound of a break-in?
12. Gusto
13. Risotto veggie
14. Knot
15. Acquire through work
16. _____ Country Buffet
17. Cap-and-gowner
18. 1993 Billy Joel album
21. "The _____ Star" (1957 film)
22. Rapper _____ Wayne
23. NBC sportscaster Bob
26. Iago's wife
30. Theater award
31. Team now of Brooklyn
32. "Arabian Nights" sailor
35. They can be grand
37. Chemical suffix
38. Leon Uris book, with "The"
39. "El Cantante" star
46. Part of et al.
47. Gershwin brother
48. Fill a freighter
49. "Buddenbrooks" author Thomas
50. "Illmatic" rapper
51. Fleming and McEwan
52. Wade with difficulty
53. Suffix for computer
54. Part of QED

DOWN

1. "In Heaven There Is No _____"
2. Jai _____
3. Sportscaster Albert
4. "Being Julia" star
5. Flatware items
6. Women's magazine
7. Walk like a duck
8. "Changeling" star
9. Lively Israeli dance
10. Mild cheese
11. RNs dispense them
19. Creek
20. Cager's target
23. Romaine
24. _____-Wan Kenobi

25. Confession topic
27. Novelist Deighton
28. "Who am _____ say?"
29. Lummox
33. "Joyful Girl" singer DiFranco
34. Emulate Webster
35. Put into words
36. Adjective-forming suffix

39. Smucker's selections
40. Ben Gurion carrier
41. "The Godfather" composer Rota
42. Important times
43. Talk-show host Jack
44. Everage of "Nicholas Nickleby"
45. Joie de vivre

86 | As a Formality

ACROSS

1. Compact item?
5. Point de Gaze, for one
9. "To Wong _____, Thanks for Everything, Julie Newmar"
12. Harvard rival
13. Julia's Oscar-winning role
14. Musical actress Salonga
15. "Godfrey Daniels!"
16. Creature with a long tongue
18. Formal fight?
20. Tried partner
21. Business magazine
22. Body-shop figure
24. Charlton Heston was its pres.
26. From the top
30. Formal falderal?
34. Crime boss
35. Trophy form
36. Microscopic
37. Short-billed songbird
40. Brewed beverages
42. Formal vehicle?

46. Kind of invoice
48. Fabled racer
49. Chit
50. Fraulein's refusal
51. Fleecy females
52. S. E. Hinton novel
53. Hunt for
54. Card game with a 32-card deck

DOWN

1. Changed the color of
2. Venetian villain
3. Desk feature, sometimes
4. Lebanon symbol
5. G8 summit meeting attendees
6. Kuwaiti, e.g.
7. Botanical tendrils
8. Conclude with
9. Criticism
10. "The Strife Is _____, the Battle Done" (hymn)
11. Bucket material
17. Word in many Grammy categories

19. Pioneering Soviet spacecraft series
22. Mail Boxes _____
23. _____ Na Na
25. Pro Bowl side
27. Scoop searcher
28. Palindromic preposition
29. Zed predecessor
31. Wallpaper design
32. Have more stripes, say
33. Newspaper page
38. Clickable pictures
39. Outside hoops shot
41. Fire remnants
42. Cajun-cooking thickener
43. Philippe's steady
44. Zone
45. "Batman" star
46. Racetrack station
47. "Dizzy" singer Tommy

87 | They Have Eyes but Do Not See

ACROSS

1. Twist out of shape
5. Twist an arm
9. Señor suffix
12. "American _____"
13. Just born
15. Breakfast food made with spuds
17. Distinctive time
18. One settling a score
19. Muscle injuries
22. Chowderhead
23. Vacation excursions
25. Neighbor of Switz.
26. Embroidery on canvas
30. Catch some rays
31. Locust group
32. Prefix with type
35. Gets testy
39. Bends down
41. Jessica of "Driving Miss Daisy"
42. Light with a glass chimney
45. Phone call opener
46. Buffalo's lake
47. "That's right"
48. Put in the overhead rack
49. Becomes Jell-O

DOWN

1. Uses a towel
2. Make one's own
3. Palindromic machine part
4. Appease
5. Game with "Reverse" cards
6. Exerciser's unit
7. Prod into action
8. The blahs
9. Dressing choice
10. Food to go
11. Warnings
14. Got an A on
16. Last stop before home
20. Rock musician Lofgren
21. Erupts

24. Length of time
26. Take care of
27. Extended performances
28. Make a speech
29. Runs through
30. Walk nonchalantly
33. Time in Mexico
34. Long stories

36. Catch in a trap
37. Confess
38. Uses a keyboard
40. Inverness inhabitant, e.g.
43. "Much _____ About Nothing"
44. Right from the factory

Answers

1 | Which Way Is Which?

```
HERA  AWL  UHOH
OPUS  HOI  RUNE
LEFTWING  UTAH
DEFER   HUG
   RIGHTGUARD
ORR  TAO  HANOI
POOH  IRK  YOUR
ALOOF  NIP  NET
LEFTUNSAID
   FRO   TOSCA
WACO  RIGHTNOW
EXPO  TRY  EAVE
BERT  HEM  SPED
```

2 | Ma Chérie

```
STIR  SPA  PLAN
PATH  PEZ  AIRY
ACEY  ENTRYFEE
MOMMIEDEAREST
    END   CHA
BOG  REC  TGIF
MOTHEROFPEARL
WHOA  GOO  SKY
   MPS  MOE
IREMEMBERMAMA
REDONION  APEX
OPEC  LAT  ISEE
CONK  ERS  LOTS
```

3 | Not True!

```
DOG  WAGE  RIOT
ODE  EGAD  ECHO
DONTBELIEVEIT
OREOS  STY  DOE
    OTT  SEA
MEN  EAT  PAUL
UTTERNONSENSE
DAHL  PAN  DAD
   MID  PIE
MOP  TAB  FERMI
ATISSUEOFLIES
ITCH  BAAL  CAL
NOTE  SURE  OLE
```

4 | Celebrity Crossword

```
MISC  LAS  CLAM
ODOR  ELI  AARE
ALLI  NIN  TWIN
NEESON  GLENDA
   PRO  LOB
MARIAN  ELLERY
OLIN      ARIE
SEAGAL  PANAMA
   LIE  ORC
HAROLD  MCHALE
AVIV  GAP  ELIA
LOVE  ERE  TOOT
ONER  RIO  TENS
```

5 | Book 'Em!

```
MIST  ARGONAUT
ANTE  READABLE
SCAN  DETONATE
HARDCOVER
   AREA  LOOM
LIARS  SUMATRA
INCITE  XAVIER
CONCERT  SASSY
KNEE  EASE
   PAPERBACK
SIGNEDIN  LOON
ARMORERS  INDO
WETNURSE  PEAT
```

6 | Greek to Me

```
AVE  BAWL  AVOW
FIN  LUAU  BARE
FCC  TRIM  ENID
ETAS  ALPHADOG
COSTS  SOMALI
TREAT  CUR  LEE
   BETAMAX
BOO  LET  CREDO
URSULA  EAGER
GAMMARAY  YOGI
GLOB  GRAB  IRE
ELSE  AIRY  SEN
DYER  SANE  MET
```

7 | In Touch with the Feminine Side

```
PCS CHEST RIB
ARA HOLEINONE
PAULAGIAMATTI
ANTI STEPHEN
SEEFIT SING
ERASER RTS
ERICABANA
FUN STMARY
ANNO YELPED
EBONIES OREO
ROBERTADENIRO
ILLGOTTEN EIN
ETE NESTS DEE
```

8 | But First, an Aperitif!

```
SAMBUCA SWIPE
PLEASED MINUS
OLDHAND AZTEC
TOE SEAR ERA
STARBURST NIP
HIS PADDLE
BAGEL LOSER
ANNALS FEE
PTA GOTACROSS
TOR ABET RHO
INLET SHEARER
SIEGE LOOPIER
TODOS AMNESTY
```

9 | For the Record

```
MARK LAM WINS
ALOE ONE AREA
HOMERUNS FAWN
TONE APE
EDIT AROMA
BAS SOAR PER
HITTINGSTREAK
ADO STAT ANT
TENSE SIFT
PEA AIDE
BABA SHUTOUTS
ALAN HES NANA
HITS YEA SLAM
```

10 | Romantic Reads

```
HEFT CPR SCAT
OREO REO HOBO
PRETZELS EWER
STEEPLEHILL
BEE OAK
ETTA LIL ALA
GINGERBLOSSOM
GET TAJ OKAY
UNI SUM
KIMANIPRESS
GARB BOILDOWN
EVER OWE ARIA
NASA WAD YEGG
```

11 | From Stage to Screen

```
ELAH RIM EDIE
PACE ADO SOLE
EMMA GODSPELL
EBERT EAR ALA
DREAMGIRLS
GAP ALS TEAL
INA PITTS EVA
SNUB RIO DAY
HELLODOLLY
ORR OASIS
SHOWBOAT NONE
CANE VAN KITE
IGOR EAT SLOP
```

12 | Fit to Be Tied

```
OOH HAHA DOJ
KAA ATOM GAPE
SKIPROPE EDEN
RIPPINGYARN
NAPPY ASSAY
AMI FALSE
HANGBYATHREAD
NAIAD NIP
SOFAR SOILS
THIRDSTRING
EARL ACADEMIC
PREY ABLE ALA
SAD BYES SKY
```

13 | Echoes

```
PEEL AWOL ABS
AMMO MIDI RIO
SIMONANDSIMON
 TYPO  LADY
  SCARY TBSP
CON EVE PARKA
AGAINANDAGAIN
GLINT ANN TNT
YELP PLAZA
 GEAR  ELLA
ROUNDANDROUND
HAN DYED UNTO
OKS SSTS DAIS
```

14 | A Night at the Movies

```
TURF STU BABS
ALAR ERR UCLA
PLIE SIS TRON
SANDRABULLOCK
   DOM LEE
SWAYZE ADRIEN
AHA     MVP
NORMAL REAPER
   AGE OAR
ASHTONKUTCHER
DEAL NOR HERO
DEMI ORK ERIC
SPAN NNE REEK
```

15 | Crossword for Dummies

```
DIVA DDT FOPS
OVERTOOK ODIE
VENTRILOQUIST
EST INT ULNAS
  JOG DES
WHEE CUE FEZ
AUCTIONBRIDGE
GTO SAN IRON
  GAR TAI
GHANA PAC DIS
AUTOCRASHTEST
SLIM BAKESALE
HATE IRS PREP
```

16 | Say "I Do"

```
FIJI KLM WUSS
BOOM LOO IHOP
INTO ACTALONE
  GETHITCHED
ASSETS FAO
SPINACH AIR
TAKETHEPLUNGE
ASH  HOISTED
 SPF INSETS
TIETHEKNOT
BOXEDSET EPEE
SWIM TEA EGGS
PATS APT LAOS
```

17 | Comfort Foods

```
TAPS ASH FAST
ARIA GEE RIPE
ICECREAM ISIN
   ARM PELTS
AVERT ABUSES
MIRA SNIP
PEANUT BUTTER
  KISS AURA
ALBERT CREEP
ALIAS EVA
LINC MEATLOAF
UNDO ELI IDLE
MEAN DEN DEED
```

18 | Duke It Out

```
STUB ETC MEOW
OUZO RAH ANNE
BRIG SMACKDAB
ENSUE MOE
  SOCKPUPPET
BET NAY PARTY
USED PSI ROCK
RANUP EVE SHE
PUNCHPRESS
  HIE POOCH
BOXELDER FARE
INKS RAY AHEM
ZEES ORE SUES
```

19 | Jennifer Who?

```
SUDS ■ CLEARSUP
ABIT ■ COMPACTS
LOPEZCAPRIATI
TASTE ■■■ NES
STY ■ SADE ■ DDR
■ ITSON ■ UAL
HUDSONTILLY
APE ■ NEEDY ■■
IRA ■ GERI ■ JON
BRA ■■■ NIECE
ANISTONGARNER
YESSIREE ■ EGAD
STEWMEAT ■ SANS
```

20 | Island Getaway

```
DISC ■ CHIC ■ MAD
USER ■ RAGA ■ ICE
GALAPAGOS ■ NUB
■■ NAB ■ TAHITI
AGAIN ■■ BESET
MADAGASCAR
PBS ■ LEO ■ FAN
■ PUERTORICO
IBSEN ■■ SOBER
HAWAII ■ ALA
ANA ■ SANTORINI
VAN ■ OMAR ■ EDEN
ELK ■ NAPA ■ DAWN
```

21 | Holiday Traditions

```
RNS ■ GPS ■ SALSA
OOP ■ IRA ■ TROLL
OAR ■ NON ■ ERROL
THANKSGIVING
■ SWIG ■ RED
HALLOWEEN ■ AIL
ORES ■ ERA ■ AINT
OKD ■ MARDIGRAS
■ EAR ■ SEEP
CHRISTMASDAY
GIANT ■ RIB ■ ANA
MARIA ■ ACE ■ LIN
TOMEI ■ PAL ■ ECG
```

22 | Just a Suggestion

```
PIE ■ ASKEW ■ IDO
ADS ■ SLATE ■ DEB
WITHOUTATRACE
■ ORANGE ■ AHAS
STATE ■ CAJOLE
KID ■ GRETA
ICANTAKEAHINT
■ AUTOS ■ NUN
ACTONE ■ MADAT
WHIM ■ OREGON
FEMININETOUCH
USE ■ IRENE ■ BEE
LTD ■ LASTS ■ TDS
```

23 | Powder Room

```
MASH ■ JAW ■ PEKE
RATE ■ OLE ■ ORAL
SARI ■ BABYTALK
■ IDO ■ ESSES
BAKINGDISH
ARE ■ ERIN ■ OBEY
SLUR ■ ONA ■ TALE
HOPE ■ WELL ■ NBA
■ GUNSLINGER
ARNAZ ■ POE
CHILIDOG ■ IDLE
TONI ■ IRA ■ SOIL
ASEA ■ GEL ■ ENDS
```

24 | Out of Brooklyn

```
TOTAL ■ PEG ■ ADD
SPIRO ■ ALI ■ SEE
PATER ■ LBJ ■ TAB
■ HONEYMOONERS
■ ALA ■ WEAR
VHS ■ ELK ■ SIRE
JACKIEGLEASON
SLOE ■ BAN ■ KID
■ WETS ■ LEA
RALPHKRAMDEN
OUI ■ RUE ■ IMPEL
URN ■ OLD ■ EIEIO
TAG ■ ELS ■ STENT
```

25 | Wok-aholic

```
JONAH ABA SHE
OPINE LES REX
KUNGPAOSHRIMP
ESAU SEE ALSO
    IRK EDNA
ABASE OCA NEO
CASHEWCHICKEN
TAP SIT SHALE
  IRED NYE
OKRA EAT ASPS
BEIJINGHOTPOT
INN DEE DERMA
TOG ADD DRYER
```

26 | Don't Fail Me Now!

```
PASS DIS SWAB
LULL UMP PILE
ARIA MBA ALBS
TAMP DUD DAT
  SQUEEGEE
ASP UMS RAYON
SHADES SERENE
KEPIS THE DEW
  ENTREATS
PER EEK ALMS
IRES PHI LIEU
OGRE OER ASAP
NOSE TEA DADS
```

27 | Profits in Baskets

```
VISE DISH GAB
OCHS OREO UNE
DEEPSLEEP IND
KIDNAP MEANER
ANS WHEE BETE
  OFID YEATS
NOTHINGBUTNET
ONEAT ALPS
NLER PREP CAD
SENATE AIELLO
KAI EASTEREGG
IVE ACRE MAAM
DER REID AREA
```

28 | Football's Famous Brothers

```
MACS BECK SSW
ARAT LULU ONA
SOME ARAB LAX
SUPERBOWLMVP
ASIDE AMES
GEO ARCHIE
EDNA EDU SNOB
  PASSES OVA
ABET PACED
MAXWELLAWARD
QBS OLEO ANTI
EEK RING IDLE
DRS KATE TOYS
```

29 | Relax!

```
ORB SPOT SKIT
IOU WAVY PIKE
LOOSENUP ICES
STYLE MEERKAT
  ITS CRAB
PACT THAILAND
ADA ERASE CON
MOLDIEST OKRA
  MIRE SAP
GADGETS LARGO
ALOE CHILLOUT
NEWS AONE ART
GENT ROSY DUO
```

30 | Cha-Ching

```
CRAPE HBO MAR
RISEN ILL ERA
OCTET GOLIATH
CHOKECHAIN
  SRO TEAMUP
APP EMU WORE
CHEDDARCHEESE
MITE LOO SAP
ELECTS PTS
  CHEVYCHASE
JAKARTA AORTA
AHI ETS KALES
WAD WOE ELOPE
```

31 | Toot Toot

```
CLARO  AHA  EVE
RAVEN  LES  LET
EVENT  ULYSSES
EARTRUMPET
   SIR  STABLE
ALA  AGO  SUIT
LITTLEBIGHORN
META  IDO  YEA
SNARLS  LAP
   DAILYBUGLE
CALYPSO  OREOS
ODE  ESS  USEUP
BOG  LYE  TESTY
```

32 | Triple Jump

```
LANS  AMAT  SAW
BLOC  LODE  IRE
JEER  IDLE  ZEE
   LAMBEAULEAP
     PEA  IPO
ACE  OBI   CHAT
HOMEWARDBOUND
SMUG  KIA  DDS
     GTI  OLE
IRISHSPRING
TOM  ELLA  VICI
CPA  MAAM  OLAN
HEX  ESTA  YANK
```

33 | Where Is She?

```
APED  YES  AARP
RODE  OAK  DDAY
MISSOURI  EMIR
   ERR  SPINE
MADRE  FEATS
ALIT  GALS  SCH
ITS  AMISS  IRA
MOM  LARA  NOAH
  IVANS  HENNA
BASIS  NEW
ELSE  NEARMISS
ROAR  ALP  ARIA
GELS  PIE  NERO
```

34 | Women of Mystery

```
FOB  APT  FOCAL
IKE  ROE  EBONY
GRAFTON  LORNE
SAKI  PULLIN
   THERE  SWAT
MAC  EDEN  TERI
ETHAN   OSLIN
TORN  ATRA  LAY
EPIC  CAIRO
  SHUTUP  LEAF
OTTOS  RENDELL
NAIVE  USA  LOU
OBEYS  STY  SEE
```

35 | Ain't It Grand?

```
BOSC  ACDC  FRY
INTL  RHEA  LIE
OKRA  MARSHALL
SPARKS  IMPEL
   TIA  LENS
THEFTAUTO  OBI
LOGY  MAA  SLOB
COY  COULEEDAM
   MOSS  CAP
ESTOP  IOWANS
CHAMPION  ERIC
HOC  EWOK  ETNA
OOH  ROOS  DYAD
```

36 | Gene Kelly

```
PAD  DNA  PEAR
OBI  LAOS  ARLO
LES  ANTI  ROAD
CYDCHARISSE
SPOUSE  TIS
ALUM  SIC  ICE
DONALDOCONNOR
APT  AOL  EARL
   MIN  BRONTE
JUDYGARLAND
ARUG  HEAP  OUR
IDEA  UNIT  USA
LULL  EER  TEM
```

37 | Bea Plus

```
W I S C   D E P P   E M T
E C R U   I S A S   X O O
B E A R K E L L Y   H B O
      B E D   M C C A I N
A N G   I H S   H A U L S
B E A K R A T I O N S
C U R E   R U T   I T I S
  B E A D B A T T E R Y
S T A L L   S I R   D E S
T O N S I L   N E T
R O Z   B E A T S H I R T
O T O   I T E M   A T O M
M S S   S O R E   T O N I
```

38 | Canine Anagrams

```
M E L T   F I L M   E V A
E L I A   A R L O   N E W
D A L M A T I A N   G E L
E N T E R   S M E A R
A D S   G R E A T D A N E
      D O E S   O V E R
A D D E N D   C A R E E R
M E A N   R O V E
P E K I N G E S E   A D A
    O M A H A   R A Z O R
J U T   D A C H S H U N D
E T A   I N T O   A R N O
T E N   R A S P   B E A R
```

39 | First Ladies First

```
S C U M   F E M   W H O M
O H N O   A L E   A E R O
P A T R I C I A N I X O N
P R I E S T   T O T
Y S L   L U C Y H A Y E S
    S E A R   O B A M A
D A R T   L E D   I M U P
O P E R A   M E A T
H E L E N T A F T   U M P
      A T E   L O I T E R
J A C K I E K E N N E D Y
A X L E   T I C   T R I O
W E E D   H A T   S O A R
```

40 | Crossing Crossings

```
P D A   C A L L   O T I S
U N D   A L O E   R E N T
M A D I S O N A V E N U E
I T E R A T E   A G O R A
C E D E S   G L A R E D
E S T   S A T O N
  T O B A C C O R O A D
    L O U T S   P A S
C O W A R D   B O O N E
A P A R T   L A Y E G G S
C A R N A B Y S T R E E T
T R E E   A N T E   E R E
I T S Y   A X I S   S S T
```

41 | Nobody's Spouse

```
S T I R   T R I G   H U P
C A L E   H O N E   E R E
O P E N H O U S E   A G T
F I N E A R T   S E V E N
F R E E S   T E R E S A
      P O G O   T H O M
N O T A S I N G L E O N E
O N O R   L U A U
S A U N A S   C R A C K
E R R O L   T A K E T E N
J O N   F A I R Y T A L E
O L E   I D L E   A L I E
B L Y   E E L S   G L A D
```

42 | Court Order

```
P O C K   T S K   B A M S
S N O W   H O I   U S E R
S C R A P E U P   O H I O
T E N N I S P L A Y E R
    Z E E   I R S
O K R A   A N C   H U E
R O Y A L H I G H N E S S
S I E   Y O M   A R C S
    B L T   G A P
  C H I E F J U S T I C E
A L U M   O U T S I D E R
C O M B   O N S   M E S A
T Y P O   T O Y   E A T S
```

43 | Get a Hold of Me

C	H	A	D		C	O	O			B	R	A
H	U	L	A		A	O	L		B	L	U	R
A	G	E	R		T	H	E	C	O	U	N	T
T	E	X	T	M	E	S	S	A	G	E		
			H	O	G				T	A	H	O	E
S	Y	S		P	O	E	T		R	A	N	G
L	E	T	T	E	R	W	R	I	T	I	N	G
O	L	E	O		Y	E	A	H		R	O	O
P	L	A	Y	A			D	O	S			
	M	O	B	I	L	E	P	H	O	N	E	
T	A	S	T	E	B	A	D		A	V	E	R
A	G	U	A		E	L	I		C	E	R	A
P	O	P			T	A	N		K	N	O	T

44 | Menagerie

P	A	T	H		O	W	N		A	C	E	D
O	L	E	O		F	E	E		M	A	G	I
K	E	R	M	I	T	T	H	E	F	R	O	G
E	R	R	O	R			I	N	M	A	T	E
S	T	Y		A	M	A	S	S		M	I	S
			K	N	I	T			M	I	S	T
F	E	L	I	X	T	H	E	C	A	T		
P	O	E	M		A	I	L	S				
A	O	L		H	I	R	E	S		P	C	S
S	T	R	O	U	D			I	C	I	L	Y
S	M	O	K	E	Y	T	H	E	B	E	A	R
G	A	L	A		L	E	O		E	C	R	U
O	N	L	Y		L	A	W		R	E	A	P

45 | Home Games

R	E	A	M		B	R	A			L	O	U
E	A	S	E		A	I	L	S		O	N	S
F	R	A	N	K	R	O	B	I	N	S	O	N
	S	P	U	N		T	A	R	O			
			I	R	E		S	L	A	V	E
A	H	A		F	A	R		A	R	I	D
M	I	C	K	E	Y		M	A	N	T	L	E
E	R	I	N		B	E	L		S	A	N
S	E	D	A	N		A	N	T			
	V	O	I	T		A	S	I	A		
R	O	G	E	R	S	H	O	R	N	S	B	Y
A	N	A		M	E	E	K		O	L	L	A
T	E	D		E	D	S		W	E	E	K

46 | Homophone Time

P	A	S	T	I	M	E		L	E	F	T	S
A	S	P	I	R	E	D		A	T	R	I	A
W	H	I	N	E	M	E	R	C	H	A	N	T
L	Y	N	N		O	N	O		A	N	T	E
		I	N	S			Y	A	N	K		
A	G	R	E	E		O	A	R		L	E	A
H	E	I	R	P	O	L	L	U	T	I	O	N
A	L	B		A	L	E		B	E	N	N	Y
	R	O	L	L		H	A	N				
S	M	O	G		I	O	U		S	A	V	E
H	O	A	R	S	E	T	R	A	I	N	E	R
O	N	S	E	T		T	O	R	O	N	T	O
P	A	T	S	Y		O	N	E	N	E	S	S

47 | Gooey on the Inside

D	A	M	S	E	L		S	W	I	N	G	S
O	R	I	O	L	E		P	A	C	I	N	O
J	E	L	L	Y	D	O	U	G	H	N	U	T
O	S	L	O		I	N	R	E				
			I	N	O	N		A	L	L	I
N	O	V	E	L		R	E	C	R	O	O	M
C	H	E	E	S	E		D	A	N	I	S	H
A	I	R	L	A	N	E		P	E	S	T	O
R	O	B	S		A	S	A	P			
			N	C	A	A		P	A	S	T
A	P	P	L	E	T	U	R	N	O	V	E	R
C	R	E	O	L	E		O	N	T	I	M	E
H	E	R	A	L	D		N	E	S	S	I	E

48 | Cubic Zirconia

L	I	T	H	E		T	L	C		A	S	K
P	O	B	O	X		O	O	O		Q	U	I
G	U	S	T	O		M	A	R	Q	U	I	S
A	S	P		T	U	B		E	T	A	T	S
			T	I	S		E	R	R			
P	R	I	N	C	E	S	S		J	O	Y
J	I	L	T		D	E	C		O	A	H	U
S	O	L		T	E	A	R	D	R	O	P
		S	F	O		P	O	D			
J	E	L	L	O		D	E	B		A	R	K
E	M	E	R	A	L	D		B	E	L	I	E
E	M	S		M	E	A		E	M	P	T	Y
R	Y	E		Y	A	Y		R	U	S	E	S

49 | Read All About It

```
A L P H A   M K T   Q T S
G A L E N   A E R   U A E
A N E E D   A L A M O D E
R E A L S I M P L E
        T O N     A N G S T
S R T A   T E A L   R E A
H A R P E R S B A Z A A R
O R I   N O L O   I D L E
T E M P T     U M P
    V A N I T Y F A I R
S P E C I A L   B I M B O
P A W   L P S   A L I E N
A L E   S S A   D E N T S
```

50 | Time for Bed

```
N A M E T A G   I N P U T
A M Y L A S E   C A R T E
V I O L I S T   E M O T E
E S P   E T A S   R E T
S H E E T R O C K   A R E
      M E T   T A S T E R
F L A I L     T O A D S
R O T T E N   Z E N
A N T   C O V E R G I R L
C G I   A R I A   R O E
T A R O S   A L A B A M A
A G E N T   L O C A T E D
L O S E S   S T E R E O S
```

51 | Too Good to Be True

```
E T O   C M O N   S L A P
P H R   E A V E   N O M E
O R I E N T A L   L O O K
N E G A T E       S U E
Y E A R S Y O U N G E R
M A M     I S B N
  M I R A C L E C U R E
    A L O E     E V E
C E L E B R I T Y F A D
A R I       L E A R N S
D I E T   O P E N W I D E
A M I A   W A F T   E E L
M E O W   N O T H   D R S
```

52 | You Complete Me

```
P O E M   P D F   G I R D
I A G O   E A R   E C H O
C H A T   W H O L E H O G
K U D O S   S E W
      T O T H E H I L T
H B O   U F O   R I D E R
A L E C   A N Y   Z E T A
L E I C A   K E G   A S P
F U L L B L A S T
    A B A     O O M P H
F R O M A T O Z   K I L O
L E A P   E R E   A L A S
O P T S   X K E   Y E N S
```

53 | Winter Olympics

```
C A L M   E L A M   M B A
A R E A   L E I A   E E N
N A N C Y K E R R I G A N
A L O H A     I S S U E
      O C T   B E L
A D E   H A T E   A P E S
D O R O T H Y H A M I L L
D E A N   O R A L   E L Y
      S H E   R I A
R O D E O     B L A K E
S C O T T H A M I L T O N
V H S   E I R E   E T O N
P O T   L E A N   N A L A
```

54 | Stick Together

```
W I N G I T   N O T B A D
A T E A S E   O L E A R Y
S I E S T A   M E N A C E
      P O S T A G E
C A R S   E R A   T O L D
O L E   S T A M P   B O O
R O B O T     A S I D E
P E A N U T   B U T T E R
      E N O   A S A
  B E S T F R I E N D S
T O U T   F I T   D O T O
A U R A   E N E   B R E W
I T O R   E D D   Y A W N
```

```
IHOP  BETA  FEW
CALL  AXES  ETA
BLEACHERSEATS
MOOCH CREPTUP
   EAT  ATA
ARABIAN    BUD
SECONDBALCONY
HOT     ALOHAOE
    ESP FYI
ANTIQUE  ALGAE
PEANUTGALLERY
BAD ATOM  ERIE
SPA BOSC  READ
```

```
AAA ASHE  JARS
MINUSTEN  AMAT
PRINCESS  CODE
    SHOE  LUCIE
JUT TRAPEZOID
ASOF  RITZ
NANO CUT  IONS
   GARB   SURE
BRILLIANT TAX
RETIE   OOPS
IDIG  MARQUISE
BUSH  ONSUNDAY
EXIT ISEE  EWE
```

```
AGING OFA  TAJ
LUNAR ALL  ADE
OAKIE FASHION
TRAVEL  TOO
   EDITS  AQUA
IRA YAH   RUST
PETS MEN  DIET
OBIT MES  TRY
DATA  MERCI
   SLO  FAMILY
TVSHOWS  RANEE
WET RET  AGNEW
AXE DRY  BOOKS
```

```
CBS SIAM  CHUM
ROW ERGO  HUMP
AGE MOOR  IMPS
WELLINGTON
LYLE   IRONIC
   ALSACE  ARC
WINKELPICKERS
ORB   NOBAKE
ESCROW   ELBA
   EXERLOPERS
STUB DOOR  AUK
INFO ULNA  STE
STOP PEEL  HEW
```

```
ASHE  ISEE  COY
STUB  SHUT  ABE
IAGO  TORN  RIP
FRENCHTOAST
   YAM   USED
SGT BUS  PROXY
TURKISHCOFFEE
ALIEN  ERA  FDR
GLEE   OCT
   SPANISHRICE
MOO MOMS  IDOL
GNU OAHU  CELL
MET SHOP  KATE
```

```
STP OPEN  APSE
TOO NOME  FLOW
ARP COMA  RAGE
POPULARSONG
REVUE   MISTY
EDEN  PAIL
FORYEARSONEND
   ORES   ONOR
SPEND   ALTOS
PARSONBROWN
DORA NOES  IDA
ACTS METO  NAP
SKYE ELAN  EYE
```

61 | Gone to the Dogs

```
BRANS AIL RAT
CANTO COO APR
CHIHUAHUA IRE
    PRY FUTON
PLANET TENANT
RULED DART
OGLE PUG ORAL
   DRAG BLARE
CALLER BUDGET
DRIED EAR
REV DACHSHUND
ONE ETH TASER
MAD NEO SHADE
```

64 | Hollywood Crossword

```
PUPS ARE DEAR
OHIO NIA ARNO
RUPP DOG NINA
THEHURTLOCKER
    ILE ERE
PANAMA SERENA
AGO      SUM
MERMAN BEATTY
   ALI EAR
PROJECTRUNWAY
RELO OWN ORCA
OPER LII LAHR
MOSS ENE DYED
```

62 | We Are Family

```
BMWS CHIA IQS
RAYE LEGG NUT
AUNATUREL RAP
 MOTHERTERESA
SANAA   AUDIT
AUNTIEMAME
NSA TEN SCI
  GRANNYKNOT
OPRAH  VOIDS
SISTERSLEDGE
ATV THATSALIE
GAP TERR KENS
ESS SAKS STEP
```

65 | Veggies Only

```
EDNA VAIN BEN
WOOL AGRA ALE
ELVISCOSTELLO
SEASLUG ALLEN
   TOO OLEO
ASP BUMP GOAD
CHRISSIEHYNDE
TEAR LANE SOW
 LACY FLO
EDITH VALUATE
SINEADOCONNOR
POE FILE COLA
YRS FEED ENDS
```

63 | Adorn It All!

```
SASH JET FLIP
PACE OUR LATE
CHARMBRACELET
ASTRO   EXAMS
   CORAL
STICKPIN MAZE
LOVE IDI AMEN
YOYO NOSERING
   DEFER
OLLIE   ISLES
PEARLNECKLACE
TARA ALA OSHA
SHAQ BMW WHOM
```

66 | The Paper

```
BAD BAMBI VOW
AWE INAID APE
ROB GOODTIMES
BLURB   ANON
 GOLDENGLOBE
 CUOMO ASAP
MPG EGBDF ERA
ARAB GOTIT
DISNEYWORLD
 SOAR   ECOLE
MOVIESTAR ZAP
UNE CHILE EKE
MSN TYPED NEE
```

67 | Prints Charming

```
KAY COO AQUAS
IBERIAN SURLY
DETENTE HALED
SLIMCHANTS
    AHS ORIENT
ASTI  AVA SAY
SCENTSWAYBACK
PAR OIL  RULE
STRONG ADO
    MINTSWORDS
MRBIG ATEDIRT
EARTH PRESLEY
GHOST SOB EWE
```

68 | Home Field Advantage

```
LABEL IMP CAM
ALAMO COO ODE
CITIFIELD OMS
  TRANCE  TRIS
FRI TVA MISTY
AINT EPSON
ROGERS CENTRE
NOTME  YEAR
FACTO ANA EWE
RAHS  BRITON
ORA PETCOPARK
DOS RAY MAGOO
ONE ERR SLEDS
```

69 | Cooking Wisdom

```
LUNA BRA CITE
ERAS LAS AIDE
EDIT ASTERISK
JULIACHILD
    RFK FIATS
EAR ASIS ASIA
THEFRENCHCHEF
NELL ACRE ERE
AMOUR  AMY
    BONAPPETIT
CRABCAKE MAMA
PIKE NIB EXAM
ROAD ANY NICE
```

70 | Winter Blues

```
 DAMS HARM
REMIT ALIAS
PALACE SPORTS
OIL STETS IRE
ELAL SOY GAEL
 ETON PENAL
HAVEN BREAK
NOBEL LAOS
ELSE GAR ETNA
LIT CUTIE RES
LEAGUE SQUASH
RIOTS TURNS
 NAST AILS
```

71 | Is He for Real?

```
 BARBS PIC
TOREUP ONUS
MANOFMYDREAMS
ABEL  DEXTER
SOULMATE ARLO
HOP ORR SCOT
  MRRIGHT
AWET ENO SAN
ONEA TRUELOVE
AVENUE  AROW
KINDREDSPIRIT
LIES EARNED
 ERA STEEL
```

72 | Hearing Earrings

```
CAP MASH COIF
BTU ARLO HARI
SAM STUDPOKER
TRAP IRAQI
VISORS DRRUTH
   OKAY  SOU
DROPONESGUARD
ROC  SUET
JETLAG BLAZER
   ISLES HIRE
LOOPHOLES LAM
AUDI BLTS CSI
BRED EAST HEX
```

73 | Mothers of Invention

```
LOVELACE  DRAW
ACETATES  DADA
STRUDELS  EVAL
SATIE  TEA  INK
ONES  SIXPENCE
SEX  CIC  GREER
   CUB  JAR
LABOR  BUR  EPH
ADONISES  INRE
MOP  EAR  ANTES
AREA  SLICKEST
REEL  HITHERTO
REPT  ANDERSON
```

74 | Appliance Attachments

```
SWIG  RUE  PEAS
ARNO  ANTHILLS
WAFFLEIRONMAN
SPREE   EBB
  ORGAN  OASIS
SIN  ATOP  LENA
HOTPLATEGLASS
ONOR  NERO  TOE
DAFOE  SUMAC
   GRE   ELOPE
GASRANGEROVER
NOTASOUL  HELM
PLUM  SNL  AREA
```

75 | Cave Dwellers

```
ADD  RTES  DUCK
MOO  EELS  ELLE
YOGIBEAR  SNIP
 SCOTT  OKAPI
POLYPHEMUS
OBI   SIZESUP
MIFUNE  NOTONE
PEEPERS   FDR
  THEPHANTOM
HANOI  IOTAS
OMEN  ALLEYOOP
BONO  PLEA  AHI
SKEW  PSST  POE
```

76 | Going Postal

```
WADS  JIG  AMOK
IGET  ARE  COMA
SUSANBANTHONY
HAITI    EERIE
   DEMER
AMELIAEARHART
RARE  SAT  ERIE
MARILYNMONROE
   OATER
EBSEN    AMISS
BILLIEHOLIDAY
ADAM  VOW  MOWN
YEWS  AWL  ELSE
```

77 | Charming

```
PIN  DEB  PARIS
ETE  ITA  ELITE
DECAGON  NONET
INKLING  DOGMA
  LET  LEAF
IMAC  SEAN  BBC
LOCKET  STEREO
LEE  SANE  NAAN
   SKYE  FTC
SUSHI  WHEREAS
AROOM  JEWELRY
CAMEO  ORE  EIN
SLEDS  BAR  TLC
```

78 | Ladies First

```
AMAJ  PEZ  ISMS
NINE  ELI  NEAT
INASHELL  NANO
MISSSPELL  MIR
AMAIN   IAMSAM
LUZ   ILONA
MISSCONDUCT
  TEENS   ORS
CASPER   ASNAP
HIC  MISSMATCH
AMOK  NOMINATE
MERE  KSU  DIOR
PENN  SAG  INRE
```

79 | Fancy Party Attire

80 | Double Goalposts

81 | Broadway Tunes

82 | Strictly Ballroom

83 | Gal Pals

84 | By the Hour

85 | That Certain Something

B	A	M	A		S	S	W		A	H	E	M
E	L	A	N		P	E	A		N	O	D	E
E	A	R	N		O	L	D		G	R	A	D
R	I	V	E	R	O	F	D	R	E	A	M	S
			T	I	N		L	I	L			
C	O	S	T	A	S		E	M	I	L	I	A
O	B	I	E						N	E	T	S
S	I	N	B	A	D		P	I	A	N	O	S
			E	N	E		H	A	J			
J	E	N	N	I	F	E	R	L	O	P	E	Z
A	L	I	I		I	R	A		L	A	D	E
M	A	N	N		N	A	S		I	A	N	S
S	L	O	G		E	S	E		E	R	A	T

86 | As a Formality

D	I	S	C		L	A	C	E		F	O	O
Y	A	L	E		E	R	I	N		L	E	A
E	G	A	D		A	A	R	D	V	A	R	K
D	O	N	A	L	D	B	R	O	O	K		
			T	R	U	E		I	N	C		
E	S	T		N	R	A			A	N	E	W
T	H	O	M	A	S	F	O	O	L	E	R	Y
C	A	P	O				C	U	P		W	E	E
			T	I	T		T	E	A	S		
		R	I	C	H	A	R	D	S	H	A	W
P	R	O	F	O	R	M	A		H	A	R	E
I	O	U		N	E	I	N		E	W	E	S
T	E	X		S	E	E	K		S	K	A	T

87 | They Have Eyes but Do Not See

W	A	R	P		U	R	G	E		I	T	A
I	D	O	L		N	E	O	N	A	T	A	L
P	O	T	A	T	O	P	A	N	C	A	K	E
E	P	O	C	H		D	U	E	L	E	R	
S	T	R	A	I	N	S		I	D	I	O	T
			T	R	I	P	S		A	U	S	
N	E	E	D	L	E	P	O	I	N	T		
S	U	N		S	W	A	R	M				
A	R	C	H	E		S	N	A	P	S	A	T
S	T	O	O	P	S		T	A	N	D	Y	
H	U	R	R	I	C	A	N	E	L	A	M	P
A	R	E	A	C	O	D	E		E	R	I	E
Y	E	S		S	T	O	W		S	E	T	S